WE STILL BELIEVE

Robert S. Folkenberg

WE
STILL
BELIEVE

Robert S. Folkenberg

Pacific Press Publishing Association
Boise, Idaho
Oshawa, Ontario, Canada

Edited by B. Russell Holt
Designed by Dennis Ferree
Typeset in 10/12 Century Schoolbook

All Scripture references not otherwise credited are from the New International Version.

Library of Congress Cataloging-in-Publication Data:

Folkenberg, Robert, 1941-
    We still believe: after 150 years of waiting, watching, hoping
    / Robert S. Folkenberg.
        p.   cm.
    ISBN 0-8163-1211-7
    1. Second Advent. 2. Seventh-day Adventists—Doctrines.
3. Adventists—Doctrines. 4. Sabbatarians—Doctrines. I. Title.
BX6154.F56   1994
230'.6732—dc20   93-40456
                                                        CIP

94 95 96 97 98 • 5 4 3 2 1

Contents

Introduction 7

We Still Believe . . .

1. Jesus Is Coming Soon 11

2. Jesus Will Usher in a New World Order 23

3. Jesus' Ministry in Heaven Is Cleansing Our Lives 35

4. God Has a Plan for His Church 47

5. The Sabbath Is God's Sign of Salvation 59

6. God's Law Is the Divine Standard of Conduct 69

7. The Bible Is God's Inspired Word 81

8. The Spirit of Prophecy Is God's Gift 93

9. God's Church Unites All Believers 103

10. The Great Controversy Scenario Is Real 115

Introduction

Ellen White would never have believed it. Her husband, James, even less so. J. N. Andrews, Uriah Smith, Joseph Bates, John Loughborough, S. N. Haskell—all would have been astounded.

1994? They and the other Adventist pioneers would have found it unthinkable that their beloved Seventh-day Adventist Church would be commemorating the 150th anniversary of 1844 this side of eternity. James White died in 1881. Both Andrews and Bates were also dead long before the end of the nineteenth century. Uriah Smith died in 1903, Ellen White in 1915. Even Loughborough, who lived until 1924, never dreamed we would still be here now.

All these pioneers of our faith expected the Saviour to appear in glory long before now—in fact, long before they died.

Yet we *are* still here in 1994. It has been 150 years since the Millerites preached so fervently that Jesus would appear "on or about 1843" and then fastened so expectantly, so undoubtingly, on a particular day: October 22, 1844. One hundred fifty years have passed since they experienced their great disappointment.

Most of our spiritual forebears, the men and women who founded the Seventh-day Adventist Church, had their spiritual roots in William Miller's movement. They believed with their entire beings that Jesus would appear on October 22, 1844. I don't believe we can begin to understand today how that experience affected their view of Jesus and their relationship with Him.

Imagine the anticipation they must have felt on October 21!

Imagine how *you* would feel if you were sure—beyond any possible doubt—that sometime tomorrow you would see the Saviour tear apart the clouds and descend in majesty with His holy angels! As October 21 turns into October 22, you wait excitedly, eagerly, through the dark, early-morning hours. Sleep is impossible. The sun rises. Jesus will come any moment! The hours pass. It's late morning, then noon. The afternoon begins. Where is Jesus? Finally, late afternoon arrives, and then night falls. You continue watching. He may appear at midnight. But at last midnight strikes—and Jesus has not come.

Hiram Edson, of Port Gibson, New York, was one of those who 150 years ago waited all that long October Tuesday for Jesus to appear. The words he uses to describe his despair still wrench the hearts of readers after all these years:

> We looked for our coming Lord until the clock tolled twelve at midnight. The day had then passed, and our disappointment became a certainty. Our fondest hopes and expectations were blasted, and such a spirit of weeping came over us as I never experienced before. It seemed that the loss of all earthly friends could have been no comparison. We wept, and wept, till the day dawn (Hiram Edson, "Life and Experience").

Of course, no one is alive today who experienced that terrible disappointment. The children of those who were disappointed have all died. It is barely possible that a grandchild could still be alive. It is much more likely that great-grandchildren are living today. And great-great-grandchildren. In other words, the event that so shaped the religious experience of those who in turn shaped our church is something that we today can relate to only dimly. What was so real to them seems increasingly distant and unreal to us.

As the church commemorates the 150th anniversary of October 22, 1844, it's no wonder that some are asking if we can credibly see significance in that date as the prophetic fulfillment of anything. With so much time having passed since Jesus was supposed to come, some are asking:

- Can we still have confidence that Jesus is coming "soon"?
- Can 150 years be characterized as "soon," in any sense of the word?
- Can it be possible that our critics are right and that our understanding of what happened in 1844 is nothing more than an elaborate, face-saving device without scriptural support?

These are valid questions, and I believe there are valid answers. I believe that we can, indeed, have confidence that Jesus will return soon! Not only do I believe we can expect Him to come soon, but I also believe we can rely on the other key doctrines those early Adventists hammered out during and shortly after the 1844 movement. I believe we can rely upon them here in the late twentieth century no less than our spiritual forebears could rely upon them in the nineteenth century. *WE STILL BELIEVE!* Indeed, in some respects, our faith can be stronger than ever.

That is what I believe, and in the chapters that follow, I'll share with you why I believe the passing of time has not diminished the certainty of these things. The "delay" has been long, indeed. We expected to be in the kingdom before now. But it is still true that "we have come to share in Christ if we hold firmly till the end the confidence we had at first" (Hebrews 3:14).

I have come to adopt William Miller's post-disappointment position as my own. I believe it fits today as well as it did then. After the agonizing disappointment of October 22, Miller responded to critics by saying, "I have fixed my mind upon another time, and here I mean to stand until God gives me more light.—And that is *Today,* TODAY and TODAY, until He comes" (quoted in *SDA Encyclopedia*, rev. ed., ed. Don F. Neufeld [Hagerstown, Md.: Review and Herald, 1976], 10: 891).

I recommend that position to you in 1994. Come with me as we examine the reasons why *We Still Believe.*

Chapter 1

We Still Believe . . . Jesus Is Coming Soon

In many ways, Americans living in 1844 would have been more at home in the world as it was when Jesus lived here than they would be in our world of the late twentieth century—only 150 years later.

That is not an exaggeration.

Historian Paul Johnson has called the years between 1815 and 1830 the "birth of the modern," a dividing line between the industrial age leading to today's high-tech wizardry and an earlier world that had continued unchanged in many important aspects for several thousand years. For example, the first passenger service using the newly developed steam locomotive began in 1830 between Manchester and Liverpool, England. Until then, the fastest means of travel remained the horse, just as it had since earliest times. The telegraph became a practical device in the United States in 1844 with transmission of a message between the national capital and the nearby city of Baltimore, Maryland. Before that, long-distance communication relied on the physical delivery of a written letter—basically the same system used in ancient Persia and Rome. In medical knowledge, military weaponry, industrial technology, scientific research—indeed, in almost every area—the world of 1844 was more akin to the first century than to the late twentieth century.

Arguably, technology and human knowledge have advanced to a greater degree during the last 150 years than they did during all the centuries prior to that time.

Think of what we accept as commonplace today that was undreamed of 150 years ago! Space shuttles, moon walks, and probes of distant planets. Telephones (conventional, cordless, cellular, mobile, even an image-capable variety that permits the people at both ends of the communication to see each other) with call waiting, one-button memory dialing, caller identification, and built-in answering machines. Fiber optics, computers, fax machines, televisions, compact discs, and VCRs. Automobiles, wide-body jets, antibiotics, nuclear submarines, and heat-seeking and video-guided missiles. Credit cards, supermarkets, automatic teller machines, digital stereos, microwave ovens (now in 70 percent of American homes), video cameras, open-heart surgery, air conditioning, and Nintendo games—to name a few. The pioneers of the Seventh-day Adventist Church never would have believed the world in which you and I live.

Obviously, time has continued longer than they ever thought possible. The world has developed far beyond anything they could imagine. Have we also developed beyond the simple belief of those early pioneers in a soon-coming Jesus? Can we still expect Him to come in the high-tech 1990s? Or have we outgrown such a childlike faith?

Christians in every generation have tended to feel that theirs was the last and that Jesus must surely return in their day. One reason, of course, is that we *want* Him to come soon. Another reason is that many biblical signs of His coming are general enough that each generation has been able to point to contemporary fulfillments. For example, wars, famines, lawlessness, lack of faith, and earthquakes have existed, to some degree, in all generations.

"But," say some, "these things are occurring with greater intensity today than ever before." But what level of intensity is necessary? Could not these situations conceivably continue centuries from now, in even more acute forms, if Jesus still hasn't come?

Do we have any valid reasons to believe that Jesus is actually coming in our day?

I believe our world presently faces several life-threatening circumstances never encountered by previous generations. Here are just a few reasons why it seems to me that life as we know it on our world seems doomed and Jesus must return soon.

1. World population. Note these figures showing the escalating rate of how often world population has doubled, approximately, since Jesus' day.

A.D. 1 250 million

A.D. 1700 625 million

A.D. 1850 1.1 billion

A.D. 1950 2.5 billion

A.D. 1985 4.8 billion

A.D. 2000 8.3 billion (estimated) (*Signs of the Times,* October 1985, 7).

Obviously, world population cannot long continue to double at this rate. Already, social scientists are looking with concern at the world's bloated metropolitan areas. They are tossing about such terms as "out of control," "widespread hunger and joblessness," "environmental devastation," "global instability," "violence," and "authoritarianism." *The world has never before had so many people alive at one time that their sheer numbers threatened the entire globe.*

2. Dwindling resources. As world population explodes, the ability of the planet to support such numbers diminishes—rapidly. Today, we face shortages and environmental concerns unknown even a century ago. Not everyone, even in developed countries, can continue to expect, as a matter of course, the necessary quantities of life's basic physical necessities—food, pure air, and clean water. In some cases, human-controlled factors—economics, politics, and society itself—are responsible. But even with the utmost human cooperation, it seems *we cannot continue to live as we do in the numbers that we do. Earth's physical resources cannot cope with the increasing demand and misuse.*

3. Nuclear weapons. The nuclear age dawned only about fifty years ago, yet already, two nations—the United States and what was once the Soviet Union—possess between themselves some 48,000 nuclear weapons with an explosive power thirteen million times greater than the bomb that leveled Hiroshima. A single Poseidon submarine—less than 2 percent of the United

States's total nuclear force—is able to destroy every large- and medium-size city in the former Soviet Union. In addition to the United States and Russia, a growing number of nations also belong to the "nuclear club," and still others have the potential to quickly develop nuclear arsenals.

I know that we live now in the age of *glasnost*, or openness. We are reducing our military capabilities and forging alliances with our former cold war antagonists. The world is looking to a time of "peace and safety." But I also know that human history has been an unending story of aggression and war. Peace is a fragile condition with a tenuous life. Past experience indicates that humankind will eventually use—intentionally or otherwise—the technology for killing that we have developed. It has ever been so. *Never before in history has humanity held in its hands the ability to actually destroy life as we know it on the entire planet in a matter of minutes.*

4. Fulfilled prophecy. A fourth consideration deals not so much with world conditions as with God's perspective.

The Bible presents two basic types of predictive prophecy—event-oriented predictions, such as those in Matthew 24 and in many Old Testament writings, and linear time prophecies, such as those of Daniel and Revelation. The longest of these linear time prophecies is the 2,300 days (prophetic years) of Daniel 8 and 9, which extend to the year 1844, the last fixed prophetic date in Scripture. Today, even more so than 150 years ago, the Bible tells us that we are living in the end time and that the next great prophetic happening will be the return of Jesus. The Millerites were wrong about the time for the second coming, but they were as right as they could be in determining that the time prophecies of the Bible end with 1844. Since that time, we have *walked to the end of the biblical time line. The Bible is clear that Jesus' second coming is the next major event to take place!* Ellen White calls this teaching the "keynote" of the Bible.

One of the most solemn and yet most glorious truths revealed in the Bible is that of Christ's second coming, to complete the great work of redemption. To God's pilgrim people, so long left to sojourn in "the region and shadow of death," a precious, joy-inspiring hope is given in the promise of His appearing, who is "the resurrection and the life," to "bring home again His banished." The doctrine of the second advent is the very key-note of the Sacred Scriptures. From the day when the first pair turned their sorrowing steps from Eden, the children of faith have waited the coming of the Promised One to break the destroyer's power and bring them again to the lost Paradise (*Maranatha*, 13).

The Millerites, who were so terribly disappointed in 1844, looked for Jesus to come for two reasons. First, they based their belief on the teaching of the Word. Second, they *wanted* Him to come; they longed to see Him. Both these reasons are still valid today.

Scripture clearly declares that Jesus is coming. We can agree with the pioneers on that. The question for us, then, is this: Do we *want* Him to come as badly as they did? Is our uncertainty about His coming caused, in part, at least, by our loss of a sense of urgency? Have we allowed the delay to blind us to the reality of His coming?

I would like to suggest three points to consider when dealing with the delay in Jesus' return. They do not necessarily explain why time has continued so much longer than we anticipated. But they help us put the delay into a biblical perspective that can help us preserve our certainty that He is coming.

1. God is sovereign and can choose the time He thinks best for His Son to return.

We may feel confused by the delay, just as the disciples were confused and disappointed following the crucifixion. They had a preconceived notion of what the Messiah's role would be, and when Jesus didn't follow their ideas, they didn't know what to make of it. "We had hoped that he was the one who was going to redeem Israel," they reflected (Luke 24:21). In the same way, the passing of the years may leave us wondering if we can have any sense of urgency about the return of Jesus—or whether He will come at all. But God is under no obligation to follow our expectations. He is always in control and has determined a time for Jesus' coming that will accomplish His eternal purpose: "No one knows about that day or hour, not even the angels in heaven, nor the Son, but only the Father" (Matthew 24:36).

The apostle Peter points to God's sovereignty as an important factor in dealing with the apparent delay in Jesus' return. Peter predicts that in the end time men and women will say, "Where is this 'coming' he promised? Ever since our fathers died, everything goes on as it has since the beginning of creation" (2 Peter 3:4). We have usually applied this verse to non-Christian "scoffers," and rightly so. But could it not also apply to those within the church who have begun to question the soon return of Jesus because of the time that has passed since we first began to look for Him?

And what does Peter say about those who doubt that Jesus is returning soon? They deliberately forget, he says, that in His own good time God once acted decisively to destroy the world by a flood in response to sin. And in His own good time, He will also one day judge the world by fire when His Son returns:

> By the same word the present heavens and earth are reserved for fire, being kept for the day of judgment. . . . But do not forget this one thing, dear friends: With the Lord a day is like a thousand years, and a thousand years are like a day. The Lord is not slow in keeping his promise (verses 7-9).

Peter points us to God's sovereign will and His power to act when He decides it is best. And He assures us that day will come.

We may be puzzled by the delay, but the fact is that Jesus *will come*, and He will come when God chooses for Him to come. Each year, each month, each week, each day actually brings us closer to that glorious time.

Have you ever found yourself driving home, only to discover that your gas tank is almost empty? You keep going, nervously looking for a gas station, but none appears. Each mile, you tell yourself, "I've made it this far, so I probably won't run out of gas before I get home." Of course, you know that isn't logical. Actually, you are all the more likely to run out of gas soon precisely *because* you have traveled so far. And the farther you go, the more certain it is that you will run out of gas.

In the same way, it's easy to delude ourselves by thinking, *Jesus hasn't come for the last 150 years, so the chances are good He won't do so soon*. Actually, each passing day brings His coming that much closer.

In a very real sense, we don't have to worry about the timing of the second coming. It is out of our hands. Jesus will come in God's own time, because God is in control. He is Lord of time.

2. The delay is evidence of His incredible patience and love for you and me.

The second consideration we need to be aware of is that God is waiting in love. Peter says, "The Lord is not slow in keeping his promise, as some understand slowness. He is patient with you, not wanting anyone to perish, but everyone to come to repentance" (2 Peter 3:9).

Ellen White echoes the same thought: "The reason why the Bridegroom delays is because He is longsuffering . . . not willing that any should perish. . . . O the precious longsuffering of our merciful Saviour!" (*Sons and Daughters of God*, 118).

God has always held back His judgments as long as possible in order to give us every opportunity to repent and be saved. He *will* act to destroy sin and those who insist on being identified with it, but He does so reluctantly and only after every possible appeal has been made. Even when He determined that the world must be destroyed with a flood, He waited 120 years while Noah preached repentance and salvation. When He determined that Sodom and Gomorrah had passed the limits of forbearance, He granted Abraham's repeated requests to spare the cities if only a minimal number of godly people could be found there (see Genesis 18:20-33). He deferred judgment on Israel time and again in the Old Testament—and forgave the people repeatedly when they repented and turned again to Him. And, according to Peter, the main reason Jesus has not yet returned is God's great desire to give everyone as much time as possible to be ready. He doesn't want anyone to lose out on eternal life.

Christ's parables also incorporate the concept of unanticipated delay. Recall the ten virgins, who found that the bridegroom "was a long time in coming," much longer than they had expected (Matthew 25: 1-13). The calculating, unjust steward concluded that his Master's return was "taking a long time in coming" (Luke 12:42-48).

From this perspective, the delay is evidence, not that God is unconcerned about us, but, instead, it is evidence of His incredible patience and love. We tend to focus on the fact that Jesus has not yet appeared, but we need to focus more on the fact that God is still holding open the door of mercy, inviting all to enter.

This perspective can even help us grapple with the length of the delay. In one sense, it's true that a long time has elapsed since 1844. But in the scheme of earth's history—and certainly in the scheme of God's eternity—150 years are not all that significant. Perhaps we need to shift our focus from how long it has been since 1844 to the fact that these 150 years represent only a small fraction of the time that has gone by since Creation.

Think of it like this. If the approximately six thousand years of earth's history could be compressed into a single twenty-four-hour day, the Flood would occur before eight o'clock in the morning. The Exodus would happen about 10:00 a.m. Jesus would die on the cross at approximately 4:00 in the afternoon. *And the time from 1844 to 1994 would be only thirty-six minutes— from 11:23 p.m. to 11:59 p.m.*

Seen from that standpoint, the delay doesn't seem so significant, especially when we realize that God is waiting a little longer in order to save as many as possible.

3. To be Christians means that we are called to an ongoing sense of imminence, expectation, and trust.

Here is the third factor to consider when we deal with the delay. Jesus says:

> "No one knows about that day or hour, not even the angels in heaven, nor the Son, but only the Father. Be on guard! Be alert! You do not know when that time will come. It is like a man going away: He leaves his house in charge of his servants, each with his assigned task, and tells the

one at the door to keep watch.

"Therefore keep watch, because you do not know when the owner of the house will come back—whether in the evening, or at midnight, or when the rooster crows, or at dawn. If he comes suddenly, do not let him find you sleeping. What I say to you, I say to everyone: 'Watch!' " (Mark 13:32-37).

This means we should live our lives every day as if Jesus might come at any time—as indeed He might. It also means that we should live every day as good stewards of all that God has entrusted to our care in order to make a better world. In this parable, and others, Jesus made it clear that while we are to live in expectation of His soon return, we are also to "occupy till I come" (Luke 19:13, KJV). When asked what he would do if he knew Jesus would come tomorrow, Martin Luther is supposed to have replied, "I would plant a tree today."

Both the Bible and the Spirit of Prophecy consistently present the second coming as near. Apparently, the disciples fully expected Jesus to come again in their lifetime (see Acts 1:6). The apostle Paul exhorted the Roman Christians, "The hour has come for you to wake up from your slumber, because our salvation is nearer now than when we first believed. The night is nearly over; the day is almost here" (Romans 13:11, 12). He told the Corinthian Christians, "The time is short" (1 Corinthians 7:29). At Thessalonica, some even quit their jobs in their fevered expectation of Jesus' coming, so that Paul had to warn them against fanaticism (see 2 Thessalonians 2:1-12; 3:6-13).

Ellen White writes:

The angels of God in their messages to men represent time as very short. Thus it has always been presented to me. It is true that time has continued longer than we expected in the early days of this message. Our Saviour did not appear as soon as we hoped. But has the Word of the Lord failed? Never! It should be remembered that the promises and the threatenings of God are alike conditional (*Evangelism*, 695).

How are we to live, then, in light of the fact that there has been such a long delay?

Apparently, we are not to be anxious about the time of His coming. We are to anticipate it, expect it, look for it. But at the same time we are to trust Jesus so that we continue to occupy the place and the work He has left us to do: "Therefore go and make disciples of all nations, baptizing them in the name of the Father and of the Son and of the Holy Spirit, and teaching them to obey everything I have commanded you. And surely I will be with you always, to the very end of the age" (Matthew 28:19, 20).

While we wait for Him to come, we are to live and work and witness in a way that testifies to our confidence in His love for us. We are to rest in His salvation here and now even as we anticipate the fullness of the salvation to come when He appears. The apostle John puts it this way:

How great is the love the Father has lavished on us, that we should be called children of God! And that is what we are! . . . Dear friends, now we are children of God, and what we will be has not yet been made known. But we know that when he appears, we shall be like him, for we shall see him as he is. Everyone who has this hope in him purifies himself, just as he is pure (1 John 3:1-3).

What a wonderful description of what it means to live in expectation of His appearing while trusting Him to sustain us day by day! The time *is* near. Jesus *will* come soon. Each passing day brings us closer. This is true in a very personal sense as well as in absolute terms.

How much time is left on God's clock for earth? The fact is, we simply don't know. All the indications are that Jesus will come soon. But no matter how many years earth may have in absolute terms, in a personal sense, the return of Jesus is no farther away than our last heartbeat—only decades away, at most, for any of us.

As Seventh-day Adventists, we have been concerned to uphold the biblical truth that those who die sleep in death until the resurrection at the end of time; so much so that I sometimes think we have tended to overlook another truth—the truth that in practical terms, death and eternity *do* mean virtually the same thing. Those who died in Christ last week will not realize that eternity has arrived for them sooner than for those who died in Christ 50 years ago or 150 or 1,500 years ago. For each, the next conscious moment following death will be the sight of their precious Lord returning.

It was the evening of October 22, 1991. Mother and Dad had spent a pleasant evening together in their basement study in Spokane, Washington, doing what they loved most, being together and studying the Bible and Spirit of Prophecy. Dad went upstairs to the kitchen to get one of his loose-leaf notebooks in which, over the years, he had compiled his favorite quotations. Sitting at the kitchen counter, he began to read the material he planned to share with some conference workers. When Mother came upstairs a few minutes later, she found him with his face down on the book.

Like his father before him, my father had preached the soon return of Jesus all his life. He rests now, sleeping and awaiting the call of the Life Giver. But, as far as he is concerned, the second coming will interrupt his reading. When the Lord returns and Dad is raised to eternal life, the train of Dad's thoughts will momentarily pick up where they left off. However long it may be in real time before Jesus comes, for Dad, at one moment, he will be reading a favorite quotation and the next instant, he will see his Saviour! I can hardly wait for that day to come!

Why has Jesus waited so long? We want Him to come. We long for Him to return.

I believe the primary reason for the delay is the reason we have looked at from the apostle Peter: "He is patient with you, not wanting anyone to perish, but everyone to come to repentance" (2 Peter 3:9). God is waiting in love for you and me and everyone else who will to turn to Him with all our hearts, repent of our sins, and allow Him to fill us with His righteousness. Praise the Lord for His patience and His overwhelming love! Though delayed, He will come, and come soon, for He has promised. "He who testifies to these things says, 'Yes, I am coming soon.' Amen. Come, Lord Jesus" (Revelation 22:20).

Chapter 2

We Still Believe . . . Jesus Will Usher in a New World Order

William Miller and his followers were right when they said Daniel's 2300-day prophecy would end on October 22, 1844. They were wrong, of course, when they said that on that day Jesus would come to earth the second time.

Yet they were not so completely wrong as we may have thought.

Obviously, Jesus didn't come to earth as Miller predicted. But on that date, He did come to the great judgment scene, the heavenly courtroom presided over by His Father. Here is how Daniel describes Jesus' coming to the sanctuary:

> I looked, and there before me was one like a son of man, coming with the clouds of heaven. He approached the Ancient of Days and was led into his presence. He was given authority, glory, and sovereign power; all peoples, nations, and men of every language worshiped him. His dominion is an everlasting dominion that will not pass away, and his kingdom is one that will never be destroyed (Daniel 7:13, 14).

Notice the similarities between Daniel's description of Jesus' coming to the sanctuary judgment scene in 1844 and these New Testament descriptions of His second coming to earth:

> At that time the sign of the Son of Man will appear in the sky, and all the nations of the earth will mourn. They

will see the Son of Man coming on the clouds of the sky, with power and great glory (Matthew 24:30).

To him be glory and power for ever and ever! Amen. Look, he is coming with the clouds, and every eye will see him, even those who pierced him; and all the peoples of the earth will mourn because of him (Revelation 1:6, 7).

In both events, Jesus comes with clouds. In both, He comes with glory and great power. He is called the Son of Man in both descriptions. And both comings directly affect all peoples and nations on earth.

Yes, Miller and his followers were wrong, but I believe they were more right than we often give them credit:

• They were right that something immensely significant was to happen in 1844.
• They were right that it would have a dramatic impact on the entire earth.
• They were right that it would concern Jesus and His role as humanity's Saviour.
• They were right that it involved a work of preparing to meet Him.
• And they were right that it would have eternal consequences for every person living on earth.

Ellen White describes their mistake in these words:

JESUS did not come to earth as the waiting, joyful company expected, to cleanse the Sanctuary, by purifying the earth by fire. I saw that they were correct in their reckoning of the prophetic periods. Prophetic time closed in 1844. Their mistake consisted in not understanding what the Sanctuary was, and the nature of its cleansing. JESUS did enter the Most Holy place to cleanse the Sanctuary at the ending of the days. I looked again at the waiting, disappointed company. They looked sad. They carefully examined the evidences of their faith, and followed down through the reckoning of the prophetic periods, and could discover no mistake. Time was fulfilled, but where was their Sav- iour? (*Spiritual Gifts,* 1:148, 149).

As they would come to see, their Saviour was in the Most Holy Place of the sanctuary in heaven. He came to the court- room there in 1844 to present the closing arguments that would wrap up each person's case and that would allow Him to find His clients not guilty.

No, Miller and the Millerites were not as mistaken as we have sometimes believed. Although Jesus didn't come to earth as they expected, He did begin the final phase of His saving work. His coming to the sanctuary in heaven in 1844 was nec- essary and preparatory to His return to earth in glory. The two are linked.

If this is so, it puts a new light on what Jesus is doing today in heaven. He is not simply performing some complicated ritual foreshadowed in the Old Testament sanctuary service. He also is engaged in a ministry that is a vital part of the preparation needed in order to make it possible for Him to come to earth. And what He is doing intimately involves you and me! This is what the early Adventist pioneers came to understand as the explanation for their great disappointment. And this is what we still believe today.

When Hiram Edson stopped in midcornfield the morning fol- lowing the disappointment and "saw distinctly and clearly that instead of our High Priest coming out of the Most Holy of the heavenly sanctuary to come to this earth on the tenth day of the seventh month, at the end of the 2300 days, He for the first time entered on that day the second apartment of that sanctu- ary; and that He had a work to perform in the most holy before coming to this earth," this was not a rationalization designed to save face when Jesus didn't appear as predicted (quoted in F. D. Nichol, *The Midnight Cry*, [Hagerstown, Md.: Review and Her- ald, 1944], 479). A. W. Spalding calls it a revolutionary idea, "comparable . . . to the change in concept of the nature of the Messiah's mission, which came to Christ's disciples after their disappointment at the crucifixion" (*Origin and History of*

Seventh-day Adventists [Hagerstown, Md.: Review and Herald, 1961], 1:102).

And this truly is a revolutionary concept. For if Jesus is actually engaged in His final ministry in heaven, then it becomes tremendously important for us to live each day, not only in the expectation of His coming, but also in the light of what He is doing in preparation for His return.

How should we live in view of the judgment going on in heaven? How does our understanding of Jesus' ministry that began in 1844 give added content and meaning to His coming? These are questions that we will consider further in the next chapter. However, it is significant, I believe, that the three angels' messages specifically link "the hour of [God's] judgment" with the "everlasting gospel" (Revelation 14:6, 7, KJV). It's unfortunate that we haven't focused more on this linkage.

I believe we can understand the judgment and how we are to relate ourselves to it only in the context of the everlasting gospel. Without the gospel, the judgment can become a harsh, frightening concept. Without the judgment, the gospel can become "cheap grace." We can stand in the judgment only "in Christ," in the assurance that the everlasting gospel provides.

The righteousness that qualifies us for heaven, now and in the judgment, is Christ's righteousness, which Satan cannot touch. It is not God's will that we walk on an insecure tightrope, balancing our way to heaven, unsure of whether He will open the door when we arrive. Does God invite us to "approach the throne of grace with confidence" (Hebrews 4:16) and then leave us to worry about whether He accepts us? Does Jesus say, "Whoever comes to me I will never drive away" (John 6:37), and then, when we come, leave us troubled about whether we will be turned away? Did God inspire John to say, "I write these things to you who believe in the name of the Son of God so that you may know that you have eternal life" (1 John 5:13), only to pull that security out from under us like a rug?

Some might say, "We know God is faithful. We're not insecure because of something Jesus said, but rather because of what we do! It's our sin that makes us insecure. We know that salvation was ours when we received Christ—but we've sinned since then. Where does that leave us?"

We fall into this kind of insecurity when we understand the gospel as conditional good news, as if salvation were like a game of tag: Those who've been tagged by sin and haven't had a chance to clear it when the game ends lose. Or maybe it's like a game of musical chairs: Those who wish to win must be close to a chair when the music stops, to have their last sins confessed before they die. Such an approach to salvation will leave us feeling as though we're walking a tightrope of insecurity, never sure of our standing with God.

If our salvation depends only on avoiding certain behaviors, then we will find security only as we perfectly avoid those behaviors. And the list of forbidden behaviors can grow extremely long. But if sin is more than just behavior, if it is losing faith in God, then we can find security by getting into a right relationship with God. That relationship will provide the spiritual direction we need. And it will provide assurance in Christ—for it's not the occasional good deeds or misdeeds we do that reveal our character and our relationship to Christ, but the overall balance of our words and acts, the direction they reveal our lives have taken.

Ellen White comments:

> The character is revealed by the works, not by occasional good deeds and occasional misdeeds, but by the tendency of the habitual words and acts. . . . The servant of Christ will watch unto prayer; he will be devoted, humble, meek and lowly in heart, seeking to know and do the will of God. Whereas he was once the servant of sin, he has, through the grace of God, become transformed in mind and character. He will love the day of Christ's appearing (*Signs of the Times*, 27 March 1884, 12).

The gospel is simple. We come to Jesus, confess our sins to Him, and ask Him for both faith to believe His promise that He accepts us and power to live for Him every day. He covers us with His righteousness and assures us that He will complete the work of grace He has begun in us. When we violate His standards, we can turn right to Him. He'll forgive us and give us peace. So finding peace and assurance in the judgment is not primarily a matter of producing good deeds and eliminating wrong deeds from our lives through grit and determination. It's primarily a matter of entering and maintaining a relationship with Jesus in which we submit our wills to His.

The apostle John links our relationship with Jesus directly to confidence in the day of judgment. He says that God has given us eternal life—it's in His Son. Whoever has the Son—whoever is resting in Him, in other words—has life (see 1 John 5:11-13). John points out that realizing this truth gives us confidence in approaching God (see verse 14). And more to the point, he says it also gives us "confidence on the day of judgment" (chapter 4:17).

How, then, should we be living daily now during the time of the great judgment going on in heaven prior to Jesus' coming? We should be living in quiet assurance, not in fear. We should be living victoriously in Christ, not in anxious striving for a righteousness based on our behavior.

All this I will consider in greater detail in the next chapter. Here, I want to point out that what Jesus is doing in heaven today—His ministry and the judgment that is going forward—is a precursor to His return to earth. It is a vital part of a single whole. It is as directly significant to you and me as will be His appearance at the end of time.

Sometimes, such spiritual concepts can seem somewhat nebulous and unreal, especially when they seem to take on the theological terminology and flavor of a bygone age. We need to realize that what is going on in heaven today is as real as anything that is happening on earth or in our own lives, perhaps even more real. Jesus' ministry in the heavenly sanctuary and His return to earth when that ministry is complete are heavenly realities. We are living during the one today, and I believe we will see Him coming in the clouds soon.

Jesus *will* come, as the early pioneers so ardently believed. He will come to inaugurate a "new world order" that will be unlike anything the world has known. Someday soon, you and I will live in that new world. Doesn't it make sense, then, to begin preparing now? Shouldn't we be living the kind of lives that will blend into the world to come? If Jesus were to come tomorrow, would you be happy in the new world He will bring with Him? Would your interests have to be redirected? What are the things that give you the greatest joy today? Would they travel well into heaven?

If we really examined our ideas of heaven, too many of us, I'm afraid, would have to admit we see it as something like lying on a beautiful beach in the Bahamas, reading the New York City telephone directory! The scenery is terrific, but can you imagine living like that forever? What *will* we spend our time doing there?

John, in the book of Revelation, has given us the Bible's most extensive and detailed descriptions of what God has in store for us in His new world. But have you ever noticed that he spends almost as much time telling us what it will *not* be like as he does describing its glories? There will be no tears, death, mourning, crying, or pain in God's new world, John says (see Revelation 21:4). No more sea (verse 1). No temple (verse 22). No need of the sun or moon (verse 23). No night (verse 25). Nothing impure, shameful, or deceitful (verse 27). No curse (Revelation 22:3).

Perhaps it isn't so surprising that John emphasizes what will *not* be in God's new world. After all, we probably couldn't understand if he tried to tell us about the things that *will* be there. Of course, he does describe a marvelous city, the New Jerusalem, with streets of gold and foundations of precious stones. He assures us that he and Jesus will be there. He describes a tree of life and a river of life (see Revelation 21:9–22:4). The unmistakable point is that heaven will far surpass the most satisfying moments we have ever experienced here, because it will be life as God originally intended for us to live before sin disrupted things.

When John quotes God's declaration, " 'I am making everything new!' " (Revelation 21:5), he uses a special word that helps us understand something about this beautiful new world. John uses a particular word for *new*.

When we say that something is "new," we can mean that it is

new only in terms of time—"the most recent." For example, a "new" shirt may mean the one I just bought, although I already have several others just like it. Or we can mean a thing is new in terms of quality—"fresh," "novel," "something we haven't experienced before." So we may say there is a "new" employee at the office. The same English word, *new*, must serve for both ideas. But the Greek language, which John used, has a different word for each meaning. And John selected the word meaning "new" in terms of quality—something fresh, original, never before experienced.

Life in God's new world will apparently contain much that is similar to the way we live today, but there will be a freshness about it, a vitality that will bathe even the familiar with an exhilarating newness.

Can you imagine a world where no one dies? No funerals? No cemeteries or hearses? No widows or widowers or orphans? No tears or depression?

A world where no one ever gets sick? No hospitals, medicine, doctors, or surgery? No insurance? No nursing homes? No hypodermic needles?

A world where no one ever gets angry? No wars, no armies, no guns, no nuclear missiles? And no crime, police officers, or locks? No battered wives or abused children?

A world where there is no sin? No psychiatric hospitals? No birth defects? No abortions? No divorce? No accidents? No . . .

Can you begin to see why John uses the word for a world that is qualitatively different from anything we have ever known? A world without all these things would be a different world indeed. And that is exactly the kind of new world God promises us in the final chapters of Revelation. A world like that would be wonderful even if its streets weren't paved with gold or its gates weren't made of pearl.

In fact, if we find, at last, that some of our ideas about golden streets and pearly gates have been mistaken, I don't think we'll be disappointed at all. There will be more important things to absorb our attention.

My work at the General Conference demands that I spend a great deal of time away from home—often for rather extended lengths of time. If you've ever had that experience too, you'll understand how much I look forward to coming home. The familiar neighborhood, a home-cooked meal, my study, and books. All these things are wonderful. But they aren't what I am most looking forward to as I come home after a long trip. Most important of all are people—my family, the people I love. Anita, my wife, is more important to me than the meals she cooks—as much as I enjoy them.

And Jesus feels the same way. For Jesus and for us, the most important thing about God's wonderful new world is the fact that we will be there together. As His ministry on earth was closing and Jesus was preparing to return to heaven, He told the disciples, " 'I am going there to prepare a place for you. And if I go and prepare a place for you, I will come back and take you to be with me that you also may be where I am' " (John 14:2, 3). I'm sure the disciples never forgot that promise. And neither should we.

For me, the golden streets and even the river of life pale beside the assurance of these promises: " 'Now the dwelling of God is with men, and he will live with them. They will be his people, and God himself will be with them and be their God' " (Revelation 21:3). "The throne of God and of the Lamb will be in the city, and his servants . . . will see his face" (Revelation 22:3, 4).

God will set up His throne—the center of His government for the universe—right here with us on this remade earth. God could have His capital on any of the worlds among His numberless galaxies, yet apparently He will choose earth, the one world that rebelled and has been redeemed!

We often speak of heaven as our goal. But in reality, of course, we will spend eternity on this earth, recreated and redeemed from the curse of sin. Our lives will be much too busy to get bored. We probably won't even have time to play a harp! God's wonderful new world will not be some sort of spirit existence in which nothing is very real. Paul says, "The body that is sown is perishable, it is raised imperishable; it is sown in dishonor, it is raised in glory; it is sown in weakness, it is raised in power; it is sown a natural body, it is raised a spiritual body" (1 Corinthians

15:42-44). Apparently, in the resurrection, we will not be entirely the same as we are now, but nevertheless, we will be real people with real bodies.

In God's new world, then, we will be tangible people engaged in enjoyable, satisfying tasks. Do you like to work with your hands, to tinker and make things? Just imagine having all eternity to plan and complete your projects! Do you like to figure things out, to study and learn? There's no limit to how far you can go in God's new world. You can dig into the secrets of the universe in whatever areas interest you—forever! Do you enjoy talking to people, learning from them? There, you'll be able to become acquainted with individuals from all ages of earth's history. Do you like to travel? The entire universe of God is yours for the asking! Do you enjoy exercising and feeling healthy? Your body, there, will always feel nineteen years old, even when you're a million and nineteen!

As wonderful as all this will be, life in God's new world will involve more than merely gratifying our own pleasures. No doubt we will have responsibilities and tasks to carry out. The book of Revelation suggests that we will be involved in the government of God's universe in varying capacities (see Revelation 1:6; 7:15; 20:6). Whatever your assignment, or mine, we will gain a sense of accomplishment and satisfaction in serving God and others.

As He describes the wonders to come, God tells John, " 'He who overcomes will inherit all this.' " Now that might sound discouraging at first. "How," we ask ourselves, "can I hope to overcome?"

Then we remember that Revelation also says that we overcome "by the blood of the Lamb" (12:11). We don't earn a place in God's wonderful new world. There will not be one person there who *deserves* to be there. Everyone will be there as a free gift of God's grace. Jesus says, "Blessed are those who wash their robes, that they may have the right to the tree of life and may go through the gates into the city" (Revelation 22:14). Our "right" to the tree of life and all the happiness of God's new world depends, not on our efforts, but entirely on the grace of God, who washes us in the blood of the Lamb.

Earlier in the book of Revelation, John shows a great multitude of people who were redeemed from the earth. They stand before God's throne and sing, " 'Salvation belongs to our God, who sits on the throne, and to the Lamb' " (Revelation 7:10). " 'These are they who have come out of the great tribulation; they have washed their robes . . . in the blood of the Lamb. Therefore, . . . never again will they hunger; never again will they thirst. The sun will not beat upon them, nor any scorching heat. For the Lamb . . . will be their shepherd; he will lead them to springs of living water. And God will wipe away every tear from their eyes' " (verses 14-17). All this comes as God's free gift.

And all this is coming soon! " 'Behold, I am coming soon!' " Jesus assures John, as the book of Revelation comes to a close (Revelation 22:7). "Whoever is thirsty, let him come; and whoever wishes, let him take the free gift of the water of life" (verse 17).

Revelation ends on a grand, triumphal note. Sin and sinners are no more. Righteousness and peace are everywhere. The great conflict between Satan and Jesus, between sin and righteousness, is over. "Soon," Jesus says, all this will take place.

He is preparing all this today in heaven for you. Are you thirsty just now for the water of life? Would you like to be among those who enjoy life in God's wonderful new world when Jesus comes? You can, for the invitation is given to everyone. It's for me! It's for you!

And it's a free gift of God's grace!

Chapter 3

We Still Believe . . . Jesus' Ministry in Heaven Is Cleansing Our Lives

For too many Seventh-day Adventists, the gospel is not good news.

The necessity of living each day in preparation for Jesus' coming can be tremendously intimidating. Add the fact that judgment is going on in the heavenly sanctuary, and the pressure increases exponentially. Indeed, far too many Adventists live under the shadow of the heavenly sanctuary in fear and guilt. Here is how one woman describes her impressions of what Adventists believe about the judgment taking place in heaven since 1844:

> "I was taught . . . that the judgment is going on in heaven right now, and that our names may come up at any time. We can't know when that happens, but when it does, our names are blotted out of the book of life if we are not absolutely perfect. We are lost. We won't know it, and we may keep on struggling to be perfect, even though probation has closed for us and we have no hope" (quoted in Clifford Goldstein, *False Balances*, 18, 19).

What a bleak picture of Jesus' closing ministry! No wonder so many are anxious and fearful, instead of rejoicing in the good news of salvation. I'd be fearful, too, if I believed this picture accurately reflects what Jesus is doing in heaven today. The idea of a judgment going on now in heaven has raised questions in the minds of many:

35

• How did this understanding come about? Why do Adventists believe in a judgment in heaven before Jesus comes?

• If judgment is ongoing in heaven, can we be assured of salvation now? Or must we wait until the judgment is finished?

• Has Jesus not come yet because He is still working through the list of names that must be reviewed in the judgment?

• Is He waiting for you and me to reach some specific level of righteousness before He can come again?

These questions still reverberate throughout the Seventh-day Adventist Church 150 years after 1844, adding to the confusion and the fear. How do we fit all the pieces together?

In the dark days following the Great Disappointment, the Millerite movement fragmented. Some—perhaps the majority—repudiated their faith in the return of Jesus. Others recalculated the prophetic times and arrived at new dates in the future for His appearing. Others veered off into fanaticism after declaring that He had come *spiritually* on October 22. Still others could discover no flaw in the date and came to understand that the sanctuary to be cleansed at the end of the 2,300 days was the heavenly sanctuary—not the earth, as Miller had supposed. This group, of course, would eventually form the Seventh-day Adventist Church.

Gradually they pieced together the biblical evidence that explained the disappointment to their satisfaction. They came to realize that on October 22, 1844, Jesus had come to the Most Holy Place of the sanctuary in heaven, as depicted in Daniel 7:13, 14. There, He had begun a work of judgment—of cleansing—that was a necessary preparation for His return to earth. This understanding of the ministry Jesus began in 1844 not only explained their disappointment but also focused their witnessing. Their message was still the soon return of Jesus, but now it had the added element of His judgment ministry in the heavenly sanctuary before He would come the second time.

As the doctrinal outlines of their beliefs emerged, these believers came to see their work for the world distilled in the three angels' messages of Revelation 14. Indeed, this identification became so complete that we still use the phrase *the three angels' messages* as a sort of shorthand for the entire body of beliefs this church holds and shares with the world. It is extremely significant, I believe, that the first angel's message in Revelation 14:6, 7 specifically links "the hour of his [God's] judgment" with "the everlasting gospel." This tells me that if we fear the judgment, we do so because we have divorced it from its natural setting in the gospel. For most of us, the idea of judgment tends to bring to mind negative images of courtrooms, trials, accusations, and condemnation. The gospel, on the other hand, connotes forgiveness, salvation, and assurance. We need to understand that the judgment is not something opposed to the gospel. The two are inseparably linked. In fact, we can fully understand one only in the context of the other. Ellen White states it this way:

> It is the mingling of judgment and mercy that makes salvation full and complete. It is the blending of the two that leads us, as we view the world's Redeemer and the law of Jehovah, to exclaim, "Thy gentleness hath made me great." We know that the gospel is a perfect and complete system, revealing the immutability of the law of God. It inspires the heart with hope, and with love for God (*SDA Bible Commentary*, 6:1072).

I believe that the reason the judgment is not good news to so many Seventh-day Adventists is that they have lost sight of its connection with the wonderful assurance to be found in the gospel. Let's look at two aspects of the judgment that ought to forever banish from our minds any dread or anxiety we might have about it.

1. Our Judge is also our Saviour. "The Father judges no one, but has entrusted all judgment to the Son" (John 5:22). Our Judge in the heavenly courtroom is also our Saviour, who died on the cross. If Jesus loved us so much that He willingly died our death—eternal death—on the cross, will He be any less concerned to show us mercy in the judgment? The Bible assures us:

We do not have a high priest who is unable to sympathize with our weaknesses, but we have one who has been tempted in every way, just as we are—yet was without sin. Let us then approach the throne of grace with confidence, so that we may receive mercy and find grace to help us in our time of need (Hebrews 4:15, 16).

Isn't that an amazing text? We can approach the Judge with confidence! Confidence in what? That we will receive mercy. And why? Because He sympathizes. He understands. He loves. He was once one with us—and continues to retain His tie with humanity forever. Ellen White added:

God has a day in which he will judge the world by that Man whom he hath ordained. All judgment is given into the hands of the Son. Christ has engaged to become the sinner's surety, but he does not engage to lessen or detract from the obligation to the divine law. . . . Christ is the star of hope (*Signs of the Times*, 13 February 1896).

Somehow the idea of judgment doesn't seem so fearful when we realize who our Judge is. How can we be afraid of Someone who loves us so intensely? Paul declares that there is nothing in heaven or earth that can separate us from God's love, exhibited in Jesus Christ. Therefore, he asks, Who can bring any charge against us? Who dares condemn us? (See Romans 8:33-39.) And John adds:

Love is made complete among us so that we will have confidence on the day of judgment. . . . There is no fear in love. But perfect love drives out fear, because fear has to do with punishment (1 John 4:17, 18).

2. Judgment vindicates as well as condemns. This is the second aspect of judgment that should take away our fear of it. After describing Jesus' arrival in the heavenly courtroom, Daniel says, "The Ancient of Days came and pronounced judgment *in* *favor of* the saints of the Most High" (Daniel 7:22, emphasis supplied). We usually think of judgment only in terms of condemnation. But judgment can vindicate or declare innocent as well as condemn. In fact, the primary purpose of the judgment going on in heaven is to declare God's people innocent of Satan's accusations. The condemnation of those opposed to God is a byproduct of the judgment. Its main purpose is to pronounce a verdict in favor of the saints.

Have you ever noticed that the psalmist is often quite eagerly looking for judgment to take place? He *wants* to be judged! "Awake, my God; decree justice. . . . Let the Lord judge the peoples. Judge me, O Lord, according to my righteousness" (Psalm 7:6, 8; see also 9:19; 26:1, 2; 43:1).

In Revelation 6:9, 10, John tells of martyrs "who had been slain because of the word of God and the testimony they had maintained. They called out in a loud voice, 'How long, Sovereign Lord, holy and true, until you judge the inhabitants of the earth and avenge our blood?' "

If you were arrested and falsely charged with armed robbery, wouldn't you be eagerly looking forward to having your day in court? Wouldn't you want to tell your story to the judge and present the evidence that would prove your innocence? You would look forward to judgment.

Judgment means condemnation for the guilty, but it means vindication for the innocent.

"Ah," you say, "that's just the problem. I'm a sinner. I *have* committed all the sins Satan accuses me of. I don't want to face judgment; how can I hope to be found innocent?"

Here is where we must keep in mind the close relationship between the judgment and the gospel. We stand in the judgment, not in our own righteousness, but in the pure righteousness of our Saviour and Judge! Rightly understood, the judgment does not produce guilt and fear, but peace in the assurance of salvation. Ellen White stresses this point:

All who have truly repented of sin, and by faith claimed the blood of Christ as their atoning sacrifice, have had pardon written against their names in the books of Heaven, and in the closing work of Judgment their sins are blotted out, and they themselves are accounted worthy of eternal life (*Spirit of Prophecy*, 4:309).

How shall we stand in the judgment? We should stand today as we shall wish to stand then. "Seek ye the Lord while he may be found, call ye upon him while he is near. Let the wicked forsake his way, and the unrighteous man his thoughts; and let him return unto the Lord, and he will have mercy upon him, and to our God, for he will abundantly pardon" (*Advent Review and Sabbath Herald*, 2 April 1889).

Notice that we stand righteous before God in the judgment the very same way that we stand righteous in His presence day by day—"in Christ." The gospel provides assurance of salvation, now and in the judgment, in the time of trouble, and right up through the grand climax, when Jesus comes.

There are Christians who believe salvation works somewhat the way electricity works in our houses. God's grace is always there, waiting in the wires, ready to accomplish its purpose. When we say Yes to God, it's like turning on the switch and flooding the room with light. We're saved. But when we sin, it's like turning off the switch. The light disappears, and so does our salvation. In that view, salvation becomes an on-and-off affair. We can never be sure of our salvation, because we can never be sure when our behavior will turn off the lights. At best, we can only hope that when we die or when our names come up in the judgment, the lights will be on, and we will have all our sins forgiven.

I believe that is an inaccurate and dangerous way of looking at the gospel. I carried the same burden for many years. Finally, I discovered that our assurance of salvation is based on God's grace by faith, not on our behavior or character development. Each sin we may commit does not turn off salvation in our lives. After we have fallen into sin, with hearts broken in repentance, we can confess our sins and trust in the sacrifice Christ made on our behalf. As John the beloved writes:

My little children, these things write I unto you, that ye sin not. And if any man sin, *we have an advocate with the Father*, Jesus Christ the righteous: and he is the propitiation for our sins: and not for ours only, but also for the sins of the whole world (1 John 2:1, 2, KJV, emphasis supplied).

The apostle Paul was one of the great preachers of the gospel. The centerpiece of his teaching regarding salvation is the concept of our complete dependence on God's mercy freely bestowed through our Saviour, Jesus Christ. Paul teaches us that Jesus so closely identified Himself with us in His humanity that we were "in Him," doing everything He did in His life and death right along with Him. Therefore, in and through Christ, we stand complete and perfect (see Romans 9:16; 1 Corinthians 6:11; Ephesians 1:3; Colossians 2:10). That is why the gospel is unconditional good news. Our assurance of salvation is based, not on our behavior, but on Christ's. Our assurance of salvation is based, not on reaching some level of character development, but on our relationship with Jesus.

If you have ever watched children develop, you know that they don't always do what you want them to do. They disobey and do foolish things—even willful things—that hurt you and cause problems. But you don't disown them when they disobey. They are still your flesh and blood. The relationship is still there. Of course, they can choose to sever that relationship and turn their backs on everything you hope and dream for them. As much as you love them, you can't force them to remain part of the family. We can make the same choice in our relationship with God. But as long as we maintain the relationship, God doesn't reject us each time we fall into sin. It's true that each sin we commit hurts Jesus and misrepresents His character, but we don't find ourselves in and out of God's family each time we sin.

"That's a dangerous teaching!" some object. "It can lead to careless living and the idea that it really isn't important to get rid of sin." Yes, the gospel is not only good news. It is also dangerous news. It can easily lead to one of two extremes, which we will call "cheap grace," on one hand, and "salvation by works" or "legalism," on the other. Both cheap grace and rigid legalism are dangerous and undermine our salvation experience. Satan little cares into which ditch we fall as long as we tumble off the road to heaven.

• **Legalism:** I must confess I've never met a Seventh-day Adventist who would describe himself or herself as a legalist. More frequently, such people, carrying an "anti-cheap-grace" banner, back themselves into the other extreme, falling into the ditch of "conditional justification" and sacrificing the peace of mind that is born of assurance in Christ. They are concerned that if we stress the assurance to be found in Christ, we risk minimizing the importance of obedience and giving Christians the idea that they can be saved *in* their sins rather than *from* their sins. This, of course, is an aberration of the gospel. Paul wrote: "What shall we say then? Shall we continue in sin, that grace may abound? *God forbid.* How shall we, that are dead to sin, live any longer therein?" (Romans 6:1, 2, KJV, emphasis supplied). "Thanks be unto God, which always causeth us to *triumph in Christ*, and maketh manifest the savour of his knowledge by us in every place" (2 Corinthians 2:14, KJV, emphasis supplied).

• **Cheap grace:** Neither have I met a Seventh-day Adventist who claims the gospel gives him or her the freedom to continue sinning with no need for victory in Christ. More frequently, such people, carrying an "anti-legalism" banner, fall into the "cheap grace" ditch while feverishly avoiding the insecurity, Pharisaism, and critical spirit that seem to characterize those in the "legalism ditch." These people are concerned that if we stress victory over sin, our behavior (doing good deeds or avoiding bad deeds) becomes the means to, rather than the evidence of, our salvation. This, too, of course, is an aberration of the gospel, for our salvation is only in Christ. Paul instructs us:

Being justified freely by his grace through the redemption that is *in Christ Jesus* (Romans 3:24, KJV, emphasis supplied).

There is therefore now no condemnation to them which

are *in Christ Jesus*, who walk not after the flesh, but after the Spirit (Romans 8:1, KJV, emphasis supplied).

He that hath the Son hath life; and he that hath not the Son of God hath not life. These things have I written unto you that believe on the name of the Son of God; that *ye may know that ye have eternal life*, and that ye may believe on the name of the Son of God (1 John 5:12, 13, KJV, emphasis supplied).

If we stress the necessity of obedience apart from the assurance of the gospel, we risk depriving Christians of their hope of salvation. This is why so many Adventists live in fear of the judgment going on in heaven. They have heard much about the importance of obedience, but they have heard little about assurance in Christ.

Yes, it is always a danger that the assurance to be found in the gospel may be twisted into cheap grace. The safeguard against such a distortion is a love relationship with Jesus Christ and a clear understanding of what saving faith really is. Saving faith is much more than merely trusting Jesus to save us. It is always based on such a trust, but saving faith includes three vital elements:

1. *Knowing the truth as it is in Jesus.* But since head knowledge alone is not enough, saving faith will also involve . . .

2. *Believing the truth as it is in Jesus.* And genuine belief always results in action, so saving faith also includes . . .

3. *Obeying the truth as it is in Jesus.*

Our obedience can never be the basis of our salvation, but obedience is, nevertheless, a vital part of a living relationship with Jesus Christ. Every Christian who is assured of his of her salvation will be reaching toward the goal of overcoming sin— not *in order to be saved*, but because he or she *has salvation in Christ*. Rightly understood, the assurance we find in the gospel does not in any way lessen the necessity of victorious Christian living as we wait in expectation of Jesus' return. Obedience is the fruit of our relationship with our Lord (see Galatians 5:22). It simply places the "burden" on the shoulders of our Lord. We live in Christ. We obey in Christ. Our assurance of salvation is based on His performance, not our own. And as a result of that assurance, we allow Him to work out His righteousness in us.

I believe a key concept that ties together grace and law is the surrender of the will. I believe that the great struggle in the controversy between Christ and Satan lies in the battle for control of the human will. God wants me to love Him so much that I am willing to do anything He wants me to do and to refrain from anything He doesn't want me to do. My response doesn't depend on whether it makes sense to me or whether my human nature wants to do it or whether doing it will benefit me. Ellen White adds:

> All true obedience comes from the heart. It was heart work with Christ. And if we consent, He will so identify Himself with our thoughts and aims, so blend our hearts and minds into conformity to His will, that when obeying Him we shall be but carrying out our own impulses. The will, refined and sanctified, will find its highest delight in doing His service. When we know God as it is our privilege to know Him, our life will be a life of continual obedience (*The Desire of Ages*, 668).

Such a relationship by no means minimizes the importance of obedience. Rather, it places obedience on a much higher foundation than our usual limited view; it puts true obedience into the context of a love relationship. In this sense, I believe that my specific behavior is often of less importance than whether my will is surrendered to God's will. Because if my will is right, my behavior will be right—even if it's wrong!

How can that be?

It comes down to motive. If my motive is to please God in everything I do, if my will is surrendered to His will, then even when I unwittingly do something contrary to His law, my motive is still to please Him. And He accepts that misguided action, because He knows I did it from love.

Obedience is important, but the motive for obedience is more important yet. Under the law, my relationship to Jesus and judgment is one of fear. I obey to avoid condemnation and punishment or to receive a reward. Under grace, my relationship to Jesus and judgment is one of love. I obey because I love Him and appreciate what His incomprehensible goodness has already provided me. Jesus said, " 'If you love me, you will obey what I command' " (John 14:15; see also 2 Corinthians 5:14, 15).

We stand, then, in the judgment confident in Jesus—not in ourselves. We know that His righteousness has covered our sinfulness, that our Saviour is our Judge. We don't have to worry whether our name has come up yet in the heavenly courtroom. We don't have to be anxious about the judgment closing before we have had a chance to confess all our sins. We stand before God in the judgment exactly as we stand before Him day by day—in Christ. Blessed assurance, indeed!

"Let us then approach the throne of grace with confidence, so that we may receive mercy and find grace to help us in our time of need" (Hebrews 4:16).

Chapter 4

We Still Believe . . . God Has a Plan for His Church

Somewhere in the world, a new Seventh-day Adventist Christian is baptized every fifty-one seconds! More than 1,715 new converts baptized and four new congregations organized each day! In 1992, baptisms and professions of faith totalled 626,176!

The call to global mission is confronting church members around the world with the challenge of previously unentered communities and people groups on every continent. And this awareness has sparked a fervor to carry the good news of Jesus and His coming to everyone everywhere. Today, the Seventh-day Adventist Church is one of the fastest-growing Christian denominations in the world. For the last five years, we have been multiplying members at an annual growth rate of more than 6.6 percent.

Like the heart and its lifeblood, evangelism and the Seventh-day Adventist Church belong together. We have long had a zeal to share Jesus and His special truths for these last days with the world. Witnessing and sharing our faith are vital to what it means to be a Seventh-day Adventist Christian, so much so that we sometimes forget that it wasn't always this way. There was a brief time when Adventists felt their work for the world was finished, that they had no further message to give. Writing in 1861, J. H. Waggoner recalled:

> If we go back to a period of from six to nine years, we find the believers in the third angel's message, few in number, very much scattered, and in no place assuming to take

47

the name of a church. Our views of the work before us were then mostly vague and indefinite, some still retaining the idea adopted by the body of Advent believers in 1844, with William Miller at their head, that our work for "the world" was finished, and that the message was confined to those of the original Advent faith. So firmly was this believed that one of our number [Waggoner himself] was nearly refused the message, the individual presenting it having doubts of the possibility of his salvation because he was not in "the '44 move" (quoted in Arthur L. White, *Ellen G. White: The Early Years 1827-1862*, [Hagerstown, Md.: 1985], vol. 1, 265, 266).

Even some years later, Adventists were unprepared to look for converts beyond the shores of North America. But weren't the three angels' messages to go to "every nation, tribe, language and people"? Didn't Jesus Himself say, "Go and make disciples of all nations" (Matthew 28:19)? How did these Adventists expect to take the message to the whole world if they confined themselves to North America?

For one thing, they sent literature to mission stations in different lands. And some felt the spirit of Jesus' gospel commission could be met by evangelizing the various immigrant groups within North America! But the missionary zeal that was gathering converts at home couldn't be restricted to North America forever. In 1874, the church sent its first official missionary, J. N. Andrews, to Switzerland. Within a few years, the message was spreading—to the rest of Europe, to Asia, Africa, South America, Australia, and around the world.

What was the engine driving this irresistible flow of the three angels' messages to "every nation, tribe, language and people"? Seventh-day Adventists have always felt a strong imperative to witness to their faith. Why do we devote such resources and energies to evangelism? Why is it so important to us?

The Millerites, of course, felt an urgency about their message because they believed Jesus was to appear in a matter of months or weeks. Early Adventists carried over that sense of urgency even after the Great Disappointment. True, Jesus hadn't come in 1844, but He was coming soon. The world needed to know. We still believe Jesus is coming soon. A sense of His imminent return fuels our desire to tell men and women everywhere the good news that will allow them to be ready when He comes.

But I believe there is another reason—a related reason—for the importance we have placed upon evangelism. It is this: As Seventh-day Adventists, we believe we have a prophetic role to play as God's remnant church in the last days. We believe God has given us a message that is of utmost importance for every person on earth before Jesus comes. I believe it is this sense of special mission that has made Seventh-day Adventists place such a high priority on evangelism.

Can the Seventh-day Adventist Church rightfully claim that it is God's remnant church? And what do we mean by such a claim?

Critics have pointed out that the phrase *remnant church* does not appear in Scripture. However, the concept of a remnant occurs over and over, from Genesis to Revelation. In every generation, God has had a remnant people, a group that has remained faithful to Him and to His truth despite apostasy of others. In Revelation 12:17, John speaks of God's faithful end-time people as "the remnant of her [the woman's] seed, which keep the commandments of God, and have the testimony of Jesus Christ" (KJV). Seventh-day Adventists identify with that description. We see ourselves as God's remnant church.

This is a bold claim, even an audacious one. It is a claim that can easily be misunderstood—both by those within the Seventh-day Adventist Church and those without. What do we mean when we say the church is God's remnant in these last days?

Perhaps we first need to define what we do *not* mean by our claim to be God's remnant church.

1. We do not mean Seventh-day Adventists are better Christians than those in other churches. Indeed, a careful examination of God's remnant people in Bible times indicates that they often fell far short of being models of God's grace. Unfortunately, there was often sin, even gross sin, among God's remnant—from Noah and his family down through New Testament days. And there is, unfortunately, sin—even gross sin—within the Seventh-day Adventist Church today. We recognize that faithful, dedicated, earnest Christians are to be found in every denomination—along with those who are less faithful.

2. We do not mean Seventh-day Adventists have a monopoly on God. God loves every human being with an infinite love—even those who don't admit He exists, much less love Him! God doesn't love Seventh-day Adventists better or more than He does others. He doesn't give special attention to our prayers over those of others. He is working in every church and in every heart to accomplish His purposes. God doesn't bless Seventh-day Adventists while neglecting His children in other churches—or in no church.

3. We do not mean that God is depending on Seventh-day Adventists alone to spread the gospel. Many other Christians take the gospel commission as seriously as we do. They, too, are working sacrificially to share the wonderful news of salvation in Christ with those who do not know Him. Surely God is blessing their efforts just as He is ours. John once asked Jesus to rebuke a man who was casting out demons in Jesus' name but who was not "one of us" (Mark 9:38). Jesus answered, "Do not stop him. . . . Whoever is not against us is for us" (verses 39, 40).

4. We do not mean only Seventh-day Adventists will be saved. Salvation depends on our relationship with Jesus, not on our relationship with a particular denomination or group. The Bible is quite clear on this (see Acts 2:21; 10:35; Romans 10:13). Church membership, whether in the Seventh-day Adventist Church or another, in and of itself will never save anyone.

What, then, *do* we mean when we say we believe Seventh-day Adventists are God's remnant people in these last days?

1. We mean God has given us a special message for the world before Jesus comes. God's remnant people throughout the ages have always had a specific, unique message for their particular generation. For Noah and his family, the message was that God intended to destroy the earth with a flood. For Abraham's descendants in Egypt, the message was the call to acknowledge the one true God of heaven. For the returnees from Babylonian captivity, the message was to avoid the idolatry and licentious worship practices of the pagans around them. For the little band of early Christians, the message was the glorious good news that the Messiah had come in the person of Jesus Christ.

And Seventh-day Adventists today believe that we, too, have a special message to share with the world in these last days. The twelfth of our twenty-seven fundamental beliefs says:

> The universal church is composed of all who truly believe in Christ, but in the last days, a time of widespread apostasy, a remnant has been called out to keep the commandments of God and the faith of Jesus. This remnant announces the arrival of the judgment hour, proclaims salvation through Christ, and heralds the approach of His second advent. This proclamation is symbolized by the three angels of Revelation 14; it coincides with the work of judgment in heaven and results in a work of repentance and reform on earth. Every believer is called to have a personal part in this worldwide witness (General Conference Ministerial Association, comps., *Seventh-day Adventists Believe: 27 Fundamental Doctrines*, [Hagerstown, Md.: Review and Herald, 1988], 152).

We believe that God has given this church a unique end-time assignment: to proclaim the three angels' messages of Revelation 14, including (1) the arrival of the judgment in the context of the everlasting gospel, (2) the importance of keeping the commandments of God and the faith of Jesus, and (3) the imminent return of Jesus.

2. *We mean that the unique end-time message we have been given will ultimately require all people everywhere to make a decision for or against God.* God's remnant has always had "present truth" for its generation. And this truth has always been testing truth. Noah preached a coming flood, a message that required a decision. People had to choose whether to enter the ark or stay outside. Moses and Aaron presented the Egyptians with a clear-cut choice: accept the will of the God of heaven or be destroyed by the plagues. The early Christians preached a gospel that meant life to those who accepted it and death to

those who did not.

Likewise, we believe that the message God has given the Seventh-day Adventist Church to present to the world just before Jesus comes will ultimately divide the world into two groups—those who faithfully follow God and receive His seal and those who follow the beast power and receive its mark.

3. We mean that along with the special message we have been given comes a greater responsibility to live the truth as well as to witness to it. God's remnant people through the ages have often failed to live up to God's high calling. But God has forgiven and healed and reconciled and used them in spite of their failures. But at the same time, God has always held His remnant to high standards of faithfulness. Those with a special message should, by God's grace, reflect that message in their lives. Its importance should be shown in the way they live. "From everyone who has been given much, much will be demanded; and from the one who has been entrusted with much, much more will be asked" (Luke 12:48).

A real danger of claiming to be God's remnant church is spiritual pride, to think that we have an inside track with God. Instead, we need to realize that a special message only places upon us a special responsibility to faithfully carry out God's assignment—that of being the church into which all His true followers, now of many faiths and even unbelievers, will gather just before Christ returns. It makes us all the more accountable both to give the message and to live it.

Living the message and giving the message are inseparable. We cannot live it without giving it, and neither can we really give it if we aren't living it. All true witness flows out of our experience. Jesus told His disciples, "You will receive power when the Holy Spirit comes on you; and you will be my witnesses in Jerusalem, and in all Judea and Samaria, and to the ends of the earth" (Acts 1:8). A witness must have something to witness about. He or she must have experienced something, seen something, known something, in order to be a witness. How can we bear witness about an experience we have never had? All true witness must flow from our own experience with Jesus Christ.

In the New Testament church, the power of the Christians'

personal testimony, born in the peace of mind that came from their assurance of salvation in Christ and accompanied by the presence of the Holy Spirit, impelled their witness and made it effective. They knew Jesus. That is why they could witness to the power of the gospel with confidence and authority. The apostle John assures his readers:

> That . . . which we have heard, which we have seen with our eyes, which we have looked at and our hands have touched—this we proclaim concerning the Word of life. The life appeared; we have seen it and testify to it, and we proclaim to you the eternal life, which was with the Father and has appeared to us. We proclaim to you what we have seen and heard, so that you also may have fellowship with us (1 John 1:1-3).

And Peter adds:

> We did not follow cleverly invented stories when we told you about the power and coming of our Lord Jesus Christ, but we were eyewitnesses of his majesty (2 Peter 1:16).

Notice the certainty with which John and Peter bear their witness! "We proclaim to you what we have seen and heard." "We were eyewitnesses." They do not present theory. They proclaim One with whom they are personally acquainted, One whom they have themselves seen and heard.

That same experience can be ours today. It must be ours, not in the same sense in which the apostles actually saw and heard Jesus while He was on earth, but in a personal relationship with Him that is no less real.

One reason our witness is no stronger than it is, I believe, is that we tend to rely too heavily on programs and materials and not enough on a personal experience. I cannot emphasize this point too strongly: We must have something to witness about! A personal experience with the Lord Jesus Christ! Programmatic witnessing, as opposed to sharing a personal testimony to one's peace in Christ, is weak, powerless, and doomed. Certainly, methods are important. Witnessing materials have their place. But they are no substitute for personal, individual witness.

Two extreme positions regarding witnessing can be found in the church today. Both, in my opinion, take the heart out of our commission to share the three angels' messages with the world. Both are equally deadly to evangelism.

Myth 1. Witnessing is an option. Earlier in this chapter, I pointed out that Seventh-day Adventists have emphasized witnessing and evangelism from their earliest days. However, a growing number of members today seem to feel that witnessing is optional. They are content to come to church and absorb the blessings of the gospel, but they feel no need to share those blessings with others.

The truth is that witnessing is absolutely vital to a growing relationship with Jesus. Just as we cannot be healthy physically if we continually take in nourishment without expending energy in exercise, neither can we be healthy spiritually if we never give as well as receive. When Jesus miraculously fed five thousand people with only five loaves of bread and two fish, He gave the food to His disciples, and they passed it on to the people. Drawing lessons from this, Ellen White comments, "So *all* who are united to Christ will receive from Him the bread of life, the heavenly food, and impart it to others" (*The Desire of Ages*, 369, emphasis supplied). She continues:

> He [Christ] has bidden us, "Go ye into all the world, and preach the gospel to every creature." Mark 16:15. . . .
>
> The disciples were the channel of communication between Christ and the people. This should be a great encouragement to His disciples today. Christ is the great center, the source of all strength. His disciples are to receive their supplies from Him. The most intelligent, the most spiritually minded, can bestow only as they receive. Of themselves they can supply nothing for the needs of the soul. We can impart only that which we receive from Christ; and we can receive only as we impart to others. As we continue imparting, we continue to receive; and the more we impart, the more we shall receive. Thus we may be con-

stantly believing, trusting, receiving, and imparting (ibid., 369, 370).

Witnessing is not optional for the Christian. If we know Jesus personally, we will naturally want to share that wonderful experience with others. We will each witness in ways that reflect our individual personalities, but all those who know Jesus will look for opportunities to tell others about Him. Truly effective witness will flow naturally from our own daily experience in Christ. It will not be something we assume as a responsibility or a duty. It will be the almost unconscious outworking of our love relationship with Jesus Christ. Our lives will reflect Him. Our words will betray how much He means to us. Our interaction with others will be such that they cannot fail to see Jesus in us. Such personal witness is far more compelling than a one-size-fits-all program. Personal witnessing flowing from our relationship with Jesus is simply an authentic extension of what it means to be "in Christ."

Myth 2. Witnessing must involve confrontation. This is the second deadly myth that is far too prevalent in the church today regarding evangelism.

Too many Adventists have the idea that giving the "straight testimony" means attacking other Christians and pointing out their errors. Confrontational evangelism seems to be the method of choice for some. I am not suggesting that we water down the special truths God has given us to share with the world in these last days. I am suggesting that we find compassionate, positive ways to present even testing truths—and that we avoid anything that hints of an un-Christlike attitude. Paul counsels that we should be "speaking the truth in love" (Ephesians 4:15). Elsewhere, he talks about "the truth that is in Jesus" (verse 21). If Jesus is the center of all the truth we hold dear, we will not be presenting it in a harsh, confrontational spirit. We will present truth in the same way Jesus did—clearly and unmistakably, but always in love. Ellen White cautioned us:

"If it be possible, as much as lieth in you, live peaceably with all men." We can obey this admonition, and not sacrifice one principle of our faith. Satan and his host are at war with commandment keepers, and will work to bring them into trying positions. They should not by lack of discretion bring themselves there (*Testimonies for the Church*, 1:356).

God is angry with those who pursue a course to make the world hate them (ibid., 420).

Let everyone bear in mind that we are in no case to invite persecution. We are not to use harsh and cutting words. . . . Let the spirit of Christ appear. Let all be guarded in their words, lest they place those not of our faith in deadly opposition against us and give Satan an opportunity to use the unadvised words to hedge up our way (ibid., 9:244).

This is why a loving, personal witness flowing out of our individual experience with Jesus is so vital. Such a witness is winsome and appealing because it is filtered through an experience with Jesus Himself. It is when we separate "the truth" from Jesus that it becomes cold, demanding, sometimes even offensive. If we cover a city with billboards attacking other Christians, do we represent Jesus aright? I believe we *mis*represent Him and make it more difficult to reach individuals with truth. Some feel that the important element in witnessing is to be sure that we have given people "the truth," that we haven't withheld the unpopular, testing doctrines. That whether or not a person accepts our witness is not as important as whether we have done our part. I believe that it is more important to present the truth—even the testing truth—in such an attractive, appealing manner that people will be drawn to Jesus, who is the center of all truth.

Confrontational evangelism is not only ineffective; it is dangerous and damaging to the cause of Christ and to our own spiritual well-being. Ellen White counsels:

What course shall the advocates of truth pursue? They

have the unchangeable, eternal word of God, and they should reveal the fact that they have the truth as it is in Jesus. Their words must not be rugged and sharp. In their presentation of truth they must manifest the love and meekness and gentleness of Christ. Let the truth do the cutting; the word of God is as a sharp, two-edged sword and will cut its way to the heart. Those who know that they have the truth should not, by the use of harsh and severe expressions, give Satan one chance to misinterpret their spirit (*Testimonies for the Church*, 9:239).

We believe, as did our Seventh-day Adventist forebears, that this church is God's remnant church in these last days. We still believe God has given us truth that the world needs to hear before Jesus comes. Like God's remnant people in ages past, we have been given a message that will test the hearts of men and women and require them to make choices. But we must always speak the truth in love. We must lift up the Saviour and allow the incomprehensible love demonstrated in His life and death to draw sinners to Him. We cannot do the work of the Holy Spirit. It is His role to convict. Our part is to be channels through which the Spirit can impress hearts with the good news.

When Jesus lives in our hearts, He will overflow from our lives into the lives of others. I believe it is by just such a witness that God's remnant people will fulfill their unique assignment to prepare the world for Jesus' soon return.

Chapter 5

We Still Believe . . .
The Sabbath Is God's Sign of Salvation

Those disappointed Millerites who did not abandon their basic belief in the second coming were Adventists, but they were not *Seventh-day* Adventists. The truth about the Sabbath came to them over a period of time, as did the other beliefs they discovered from their in-depth study of the Scriptures and through prayer and the leading of the Holy Spirit.

In fact, when Joseph Bates began to teach the importance of the fourth commandment and to identify the Sabbath as the seventh day of the week, Ellen Harmon (she and James had not yet married) felt he was mistaken:

> In 1846, on a visit to New Bedford, Mass., I became acquainted with Bro. Joseph Bates. He was keeping the Sabbath, and urged its importance. I did not feel its importance, and thought that Bro. B. erred in dwelling upon the fourth commandment more than the other nine. But the Lord gave me a vision. I was conducted to the second vail [sic]. It was lifted, and I beheld the ark, and on it the mercy-seat. JESUS raised the cover of the ark, and I beheld the tables of stone on which the ten commandments were written. I was amazed as I saw the fourth commandment. A halo of glory was all around it; for it was the only one of the ten which points out to man who the living GOD is, the maker of heaven and earth (*Spiritual Gifts*, 2:82, 83).

Later, Ellen White described in more detail these tables of

59

stone on which God had written the Ten Commandments with His own finger. What she saw indicates the significance heaven attaches to this matter of the Sabbath:

> On one table were four [commandments], and on the other six. The four on the first table shone brighter than the other six. But the fourth, the Sabbath commandment, shone above them all; for the Sabbath was set apart to be kept in honor of God's holy name. The holy Sabbath looked glorious—a halo of glory was all around it (*Early Writings*, 32, 33).

Apparently, the fourth commandment has a greater significance, in some way, than the other nine. Why? In what way is the Sabbath commandment of supreme importance in God's law?

From its founding in the early 1860s, the Seventh-day Adventist Church has considered the Sabbath to be one of the most distinctive elements in its message for the world. In fact, when our pioneers chose a name for the new denomination, they considered several names but selected the name *Seventh-day Adventist* because it referred to two fundamental beliefs: the second coming of Jesus and the Sabbath of the fourth commandment.

We still believe today that the seventh-day Sabbath is one of the distinctive truths we are to give to the world. We believe that at the end time, the entire world will be brought to a great crisis that will revolve around the issue of the Sabbath.

What makes the Sabbath so crucial?

If, in comparison to the other commandments, the Sabbath in some way shines "above them all," there must be something more to this matter than merely identifying the correct worship day. If our Sabbath message for the world is simply to convince men and women that Saturday, not Sunday, is the right day on which to worship, then we don't have much of a message to stir their hearts. We may be able to demonstrate that we are correct, but the response in many cases will be, "So what? What difference does it make?"

Thus the challenge facing us about the Sabbath is that we

must clearly understand and be able to clearly explain why the Sabbath makes a difference, why it is so important to both God and to us. Surely the message of the Sabbath has more meaning than just being an argument over two possible days of worship!

In order to understand why the Sabbath is so significant, let's go back to those early Adventists. About the same time that they were realizing the truth of the Sabbath, they were also beginning to see that God was calling them to proclaim the three angels' messages of Revelation 14. In their minds, a clear connection tied both concepts together. The fourth commandment is the only one of the ten that deals with worship and that points to God as the Creator of heaven and earth. Thus, the first angel seems to be consciously referring to the Sabbath commandment when he says, " 'Worship him who made the heavens, the earth, the sea and the springs of water' " (Revelation 14:7).

The Sabbath, then, is part and parcel of the three angels' messages and the everlasting gospel. It is this aspect of the Sabbath—its redemptive significance—that gives it importance both for our relationship with Jesus and for the end time.

How is the Sabbath linked with the gospel?

The Sabbath is linked with the gospel because God has chosen this symbol as a sign of both His creative and His re-creative power. A sign of His perfect, finished work both in creation and redemption.

In Genesis, God set aside the Sabbath to commemorate His finished work of creation:

Thus the heavens and the earth were completed in all their vast array. By the seventh day God had finished the work he had been doing; so on the seventh day he rested from all his work. And God blessed the seventh day and made it holy, because on it he rested from all the work of creation that he had done (Genesis 2:1-3).

God had spent six days creating our world. Then, when all was complete and perfect, He rested on the seventh day. The very word *Sabbath* means "rest." Before sin, Sabbath rest was to remind men and women of God as their Creator. It was to provide for a time of special fellowship with each other and with Him. God instituted the Sabbath to commemorate His creative power. He planned that the Sabbath would remind men and women each week that He was the One who had given them life. Each week, they would rest in His love and acknowledge Him as their Creator.

After sin entered the world, the Sabbath also served to remind us of God's re-creative power in saving us from sin. Sabbath rest became illustrative of the rest we find in Christ through redemption. This is what Moses meant when he told the Israelites:

> Remember that you were slaves in Egypt and that the Lord your God brought you out of there with a mighty hand and an outstretched arm. Therefore the Lord your God has commanded you to observe the Sabbath day (Deuteronomy 5:15).

Jesus said, " 'Come to me, all you who are weary and burdened, and I will give you rest. . . . And you will find rest for your souls' " (Matthew 11:28, 29).

The Bible is clear that it was Jesus who was the active agent in creation (see John 1:1-4; Colossians 1:15, 16). The One who created our world and instituted the Sabbath is none other than Jesus, our Saviour! He made us in His image (see Genesis 1:27), and now since sin has marred that likeness, He restores His image in us through His salvation and sanctification.

In fact, the Sabbath is a special sign, He says, that His people have allowed Him to re-create them through His redeeming grace. " 'You must observe my Sabbaths. This will be a sign between me and you for the generations to come, so you may know that I am the Lord, who makes you holy' " (Exodus 31:13).

The Sabbath, then, points us to the fact that it is the Lord who saves us and makes us holy. It is the Lord who both justifies us and sanctifies us. We can do neither for ourselves. We can be delivered from the slavery of sin and grow in grace only by resting from our own works and entering His rest.

It's ironic that this symbol of our acceptance of salvation by faith is seen by most of the world as evidence of legalism. Most Sunday-keeping Christians believe that our insistence upon observing the seventh-day Sabbath is a legalistic attempt to earn our own salvation. They point to the fact that Christians are no longer under law, but under grace, as the foundation for their freedom to worship on Sunday. Evidently, we haven't been doing a very good job of making clear to the world the true significance of God's seventh-day Sabbath. Far from being an evidence of legalism, it is God's own sign of righteousness by faith and submission to His will.

Notice the symbolism of what happened at Creation. God worked six days and then rested the seventh, after His work was complete. But for Adam and Eve, the process was reversed. They first rested on the Sabbath and *then* followed it with six days of work. They had nothing to do with God's creative acts. They came on the scene at the end of Creation week. They simply received their lives from Him and all the blessings of Eden as a free gift.

In the same way, salvation comes by resting in the perfect finished work of Jesus Christ accomplished on the cross. We can receive the blessings of salvation in no other way. This is how the Sabbath rest becomes the outward sign of the glorious truth of righteousness by faith. Hebrews 4 clearly sets forth this symbolism:

> We who have believed enter that rest. . . . There remains, then, a Sabbath-rest for the people of God; for anyone who enters God's rest also rests from his own work, just as God did from his (verses 3, 9, 10).

Here, then, is the reason the fourth commandment has a special significance compared to the other nine. If we obey any of the ten from a sense of obligation only, or if we obey in order to be saved, we have misunderstood the reason God gave them to us. But this is especially true of the fourth commandment, because it is the one specifically designed to point us to the fact that we must rest in God's completed work. If we consider Sabbath keeping a requirement for salvation, we have turned the commandment on its head. We are not entering into God's rest at all. Rather, we are depending on ourselves and our works.

There are two extremes we can take toward God's holy day. One extreme is to consider observance of the seventh day a means of salvation. We keep it in order to be saved. We've already seen how futile that approach is and how it destroys the significance God designed His Sabbath to have.

The other extreme is to substitute our own day for God's day. This is what the majority of Christians have done. Sunday, or any other day, regardless of the devotional or worship activities that we celebrate, cannot contain the redemptive significance with which God has invested His Sabbath. We cannot enter into *His* rest on a day *we* have made holy.

The seventh day, pointing as it does to Jesus as both Creator and Redeemer, teaches us that we are totally dependent on Him for our lives and for our salvation. Sin says No to dependence on God. Sin insists on having its own way. That is why, when sin comes in, we either substitute our own day for God's holy Sabbath, or we insist on keeping the Sabbath in our own way and for our own reasons. Either approach destroys what God intends the Sabbath to symbolize in our lives. We cannot enter into God's rest if we are keeping the Sabbath in order to be saved. And neither can we enter His rest by worshiping on a substitute day, because it doesn't point to His perfect, finished work—either in creation or redemption.

Does this mean that sincere Sunday-keeping Christians are not experiencing Christ as their Saviour? Are they unable to find the rest Jesus has promised?

No, God accepts all sincere worship, no matter what day we observe. If the motive is right, He accepts even behavior that is wrong. Sincere Sunday-keeping Christians are observing the wrong day, but for the right reasons. I believe this is more acceptable to God than the actions of those who are keeping the right day for the wrong reasons! Both need to be invited to keep holy the right day for the right reasons. And, of course, this is what God will do for us through His Holy Spirit if we are willing to let Him lead us into all truth (see John 16:13).

Do you begin to see how the Sabbath will become the all-encompassing issue around which earth's last great conflict will revolve? If the question is merely a matter of choice between two days, it hardly seems significant enough to become the dividing line between the saved and the lost at the end of time, does it? Just to be able to prove from the Bible that we are right doesn't seem a point important enough to die for. But if the Sabbath is not just a question of which day, but rather a question of either yielding our opinions to the authority of God and resting in Jesus or, on the other hand, resting in our own works/opinions, then the issue becomes significant—significant enough to die for.

The Sabbath is not simply an arbitrary test at the end of time that will measure our loyalty to God. It becomes *the* crucial question for the whole world because of its intrinsic content as a symbol of salvation in Christ.

At the end of time, the gospel will have divided all humanity into only two groups—believers and unbelievers, those who are resting in Christ for their salvation and those who are resting in their own works. And all those who are resting in Christ will be resting on His Sabbath, which symbolizes their trust in Him for salvation. Their Sabbath keeping will be the visible sign of the righteousness they have received by faith.

In contrast, those who have deliberately rejected God's free gift of salvation will worship the dragon that gives power to the beast (see Revelation 13:3, 4). They will observe a human rest day in defiance of God's rest day. So in the end time, the real issue will not be Saturday versus Sunday. It will be salvation by faith versus salvation by works. It will be God's authority versus human opinion. The conflict will be between God's divinely appointed rest day, symbolizing salvation by faith alone, and humanity's substitute rest day, symbolizing salvation by human effort. The book of Revelation describes this conflict in terms of the seal of God versus the mark of the beast:

"If anyone worships the beast and his image and receives his mark on the forehead or on the hand, he, too, will drink of the wine of God's fury, which has been poured full strength into the cup of his wrath. . . . There is no rest day or night for those who worship the beast and his image, or for anyone who receives the mark of his name." This calls for patient endurance on the part of the saints who obey God's commandments and remain faithful to Jesus (Revelation 14:9-12).

Our pioneers realized that the first angel's message was linked to the Sabbath through its call to worship God as the Creator of heaven and earth. They saw that the third angel's message brought to view a decisive choice between worshiping the beast and receiving its mark or worshiping God in faithful obedience to His commandments. This gave them the biblical basis to proclaim the importance of God's seventh-day Sabbath.

Tragically, however, this call to faithfulness in Sabbath keeping has too often become separated from its setting in the everlasting gospel. Perhaps that is why other Christians have charged that we Seventh-day Adventists are legalists in our emphasis on the fourth commandment. And, of course, they are right, if we allow the Sabbath to be taken out of its rightful context in the gospel of Jesus Christ.

Until we rest in Him, we will not be able to truly rest on His Sabbath as He intends for us to do. We won't find the depth of meaning in it that is there. Seventh-day Adventists have predicted end-time laws prohibiting Sabbath worship on pain of death. Is your Sabbath experience something you would give your life to keep today? Would you die for your Sabbath-afternoon nap? Does the Sabbath mean that much to you? Or do you check the sunset time to see how many minutes are left as the Sabbath is coming to a close? Unless the Sabbath comes to have more significance than it does for many of us, I'm afraid we will find it difficult to maintain our faithfulness to it in the face of death.

Ellen White indicates that before Jesus comes, His people will present the Sabbath to the world in its full glory:

I saw that God had children, who do not see and keep

the Sabbath. They had not rejected the light on it. And at the commencement of the time of trouble, we were filled with the Holy Ghost as we went forth and proclaimed the Sabbath more fully. . . . And at this time God's chosen all saw clearly that we had the truth, and they came out and endured the persecution with us (*Review and Herald*, 21 July 1851).

I believe that this fuller meaning for the Sabbath is its redemptive content, its symbolism as a sign of God's completed work in us for salvation. "There remains, then, a Sabbath-rest for the people of God; for anyone who enters God's rest also rests from his own work, just as God did from his" (Hebrews 4:9, 10).

When the Sabbath becomes in our lives all that God intends it should be, we will experience such a beauty in His holy day that it will shine out of our lives and out of our witness in a way that will draw others to the Lord of the Sabbath.

Chapter 6

We Still Believe . . . God's Law Is the Divine Standard of Conduct

It is significant, I think, that various talk shows are becoming one of the most rapidly expanding segments of radio and television in North America. One format pits four or five "experts" against each other. A moderator referees the match. Another kind of talk show features celebrities who express their opinions on a wide variety of issues. Another tries to find the most bizarre guests and controversial topics and allows the studio audience to attack and defend their positions. Yet another invites telephone callers to quiz the guest or ask questions of the show's host.

I believe such shows are popular because they reflect an attitude, a mind-set, that is becoming increasingly evident in first-world society and, to some degree, in other parts of the world. It is an attitude that accepts few or no absolutes, an attitude that says, "Since there are few external standards by which to judge behavior, my opinion is as valid as yours. Indeed, for *me*, my opinion is the only validity I will accept." The multitude of voices clamoring for their right to be heard and accepted today is a symptom that society has largely rejected most forms of external authority.

Yet the "in-my-opinion" mentality that characterizes today's pluralistic—almost perniciously individualistic—society stands in sharp contrast to God's plan for the world and especially His plan for His church.

God does not expect us not to have any opinions. He does not insist that we give up our individuality. But He does expect us to recognize His authority. At Sinai, God gave Moses Ten *Commandments*, not Ten Suggestions. His law, embodied in ten grand principles for living, is anything but tentative. Even the simple words He chose have an awe-inspiring certainty about them: "You shall not steal." "You shall not kill." "You shall not commit adultery." "Honor your parents." "Remember the Sabbath and keep it holy." He listed no exceptions, no conditions. He just let the words stand in all their simplicity and with all their force. What a contrast they are to the human babbling we hear constantly on so many of the talk shows today! When Jesus came to our world in person, people marveled at His teachings, "because he taught as one who had authority" (Matthew 7:29). Jesus didn't leave a lot of room for misunderstandings.

God's ten grand principles for living are clear and decisive. Yet they are not arbitrary. God didn't decide to forbid stealing, for example, just to demonstrate His authority by telling us what to do. It isn't as though He could just as easily have commanded us to steal. These ten rules governing our lives are reflections of God's own character. When He forbids stealing, He tells us He respects the rights of individuals. He knows that if we are to be truly happy, we must bring our lives into harmony with these great principles. The Ten Commandments are as relevant to life in the twentieth century as they were three thousand years ago when God gave them to Moses.

Why, then, do so many people feel they would be better off without God's law, that life would be happier if they could just get rid of all the divine and human-made rules that complicate daily existence?

Children think, *Just wait until I'm an adult and no longer have parents or teachers to tell me what to do all the time!*

Adults, having lived a little longer, realize that we never reach the point of having no one else to tell us what to do. But adults, too, often are tempted to think how much happier they would be if they no longer had to pay attention to the restrictions of home, family, society, or even God.

It may sound appealing, on the surface, to think of living without rules. But the truth is that we can be happy—truly happy—only when we recognize that we can't always have our own way. Consider something as simple as a ballgame. Players may argue with the umpire or referee about a call or whether a runner has reached his or her goal. But the only reason they can argue is because they agree on the rules. The arguments are always about the rules, or a judgment based on those rules. In baseball, for instance, you never see players arguing that they ought to be allowed to stay at bat after three strikes. Players won't argue that they can skip second base and go directly from first to third. Every game must have rules if the participants are going to enjoy it. If everyone could make up his or her own rules as the game progressed, no one would know what was going on.

And I think the same concept applies to more than just games. Think of the chaos if everyone were free to do as he or she pleased in life. Drivers wouldn't have to stop at red lights or stay on any particular side of the roadway unless they wanted to. But, of course, accidents would increase dramatically. Bank tellers could cash your check for any amount—or just consider it a personal gift. Trash collectors might show up three days in a row—or not for three months.

And what if the laws of nature decided to play fast and loose as well? One morning your toaster works fine, because the principles of electricity are behaving themselves. But when you plug in the toaster the next day, it incinerates all the wiring in your house! What if you couldn't rely on gravity or sunlight?

Obviously, being free doesn't mean allowing everyone to do exactly as he or she pleases. In fact, that's the way to be anything but truly free.

Is it any different with God's laws, the laws that govern our spiritual lives? Not at all.

Our well-being depends on obedience to God's spiritual laws just as surely as it does on following the rules that society has agreed upon or as surely as it depends on the laws of nature. God wasn't just arbitrarily exercising His authority at Mount Sinai when He gave the Ten Commandments. He was spelling out how we need to live if we are going to be happy.

It's like the doctor who prescribes a certain medicine. God's law isn't something to make *God* feel good if we follow it. It is

His divine prescription intended to make *us* feel good, to keep us free to live happy, productive lives.

Most of us think of the choice we face in terms of "Shall I obey the law—or ignore it?" Actually, that really isn't the question. The choice we have to make is this: "What law shall I choose to obey?"

The apostle Paul points out that there are two laws: the law of righteousness and the law of sin. One is the flip side of the other. And we must choose one or the other. We are slaves either to righteousness or to sin. Paul puts it this way: "Don't you know that . . . you are slaves to the one whom you obey—whether you are slaves to sin, which leads to death, or to obedience, which leads to righteousness?" (Romans 6:16).

You see, if we decide to disobey God's law, we are really choosing to obey the law of sin and death. We are never free of laws. We always must obey one or the other.

Left to ourselves, we can obey only the law of sin. We have no power within ourselves to break out of our slavery to sin. Paul admits this in his own life:

> I know that nothing good lives in me, that is, in my sinful nature. For I have the desire to do what is good, but I cannot carry it out. . . . When I want to do good, evil is right there with me. . . . I see another law at work in the members of my body, waging war against the law of my mind and making me a prisoner of the law of sin at work within my members. What a wretched man I am! Who will rescue me from this body of death? (Romans 7:18, 21-24).

Have you ever felt that way, wanting to do right and doing wrong instead, desperately wishing for victory over sin and yet feeling it is impossible to stop sinning?

Take courage. Spiritual giants such as Paul himself have struggled with the same excruciating dilemma. "Who will rescue me from this body of death?" Paul cried out. And in the next breath, he answered his own question: "Thanks be to God— through Jesus Christ our Lord!" (verse 25).

We are all slaves to sin, and only Jesus can truly set us free.

"Everyone who sins is a slave to sin. . . . So if the Son sets you free, you will be free indeed" (John 8:34, 36).

How does He do that?

Before we look at how Jesus frees us from our slavery to the law of sin and death, let's step back and take a look at the bigger picture. We need to see how obedience and God's law fit into the whole picture of what God has in mind for us.

There are some in our church today who feel that we shouldn't spend very much time at all talking about obedience or God's law, that, instead, we ought to be emphasizing His grace and His love. I certainly agree that we can never say too much about God's grace, but why should we feel that emphasizing grace has to mean we can't talk about obedience?

As our pioneers came to understand neglected truths, especially the truth of the Sabbath, they quite naturally and correctly began to stress the importance of doing something about it. After all, if we understand that the seventh day is God's holy Sabbath and that He cares which day we keep, doesn't it then become important that we actually keep the seventh day holy? Of course. So our spiritual forebears began to stress the importance of obeying God's law—an emphasis that was understandable but that unfortunately began, after a while, to become an end in itself. That is, they did what comes so easily to us humans—they began to lose sight of the reason for obedience and to focus, instead, on obedience for its own sake.

The General Conference session of 1888 attempted to correct what some felt was an imbalance in the church. They felt that the importance the church had attached to obedience had become distorted and, in turn, was distorting members' view of salvation and the gospel. Ellen White was one who felt that the church had become sterile in its overemphasis on God's law as an end in itself. She threw herself wholeheartedly into the effort to focus more on God's grace and on the *reason* for obedience.

Two years after the historic session, the *Review and Herald* (11 March 1890) reported her words to a group of church workers:

When we leave this meeting, may it be with the truth burning in our souls like fire shut up in our bones. You will meet with those who will say, "You are too much excited over this matter. You are too much in earnest. You should not be reaching for the righteousness of Christ, and making so much of that. You should preach the law." As a people, we have preached the law until we are as dry as the hills of Gilboa that had neither dew nor rain. We must preach Christ in the law, and there will be sap and nourishment in the preaching that will be as food to the famishing flock of God. We must not trust in our own merits at all, but in the merits of Jesus of Nazareth. Our eyes must be anointed with eye-salve. We must draw nigh to God, and he will draw nigh to us, if we come in his own appointed way. O that you may go forth as the disciples did after the day of Pentecost, and then your testimony will have a living ring, and souls will be converted to God.

The 1888 discussions shifted the church's emphasis and understanding. But the effect was relatively short-lived and fell far short of accomplishing what Ellen White and others felt it should. In recent decades, the church has seen a renewed emphasis on grace and the good news of salvation by faith. This emphasis has been needed and refreshing.

However, we need to be careful that in correcting one imbalance, we don't create another. In some circles within the church today, there is a tendency to think that in order to accept the assurance of the gospel, one must repudiate God's law. Some have felt that grace is incompatible with law and that the gospel and obedience are irreconcilable.

But if we focus on God's love and leave out the ethical content that defines that love (His law), we make God one who connives with us *in* our sins rather than one who has acted decisively to save us *from* our sins. The answer is not to emphasize His love and grace less. Indeed, we need to emphasize them more. But we need to see a God who not only loves but who, because He loves, cares desperately how His people live, a God who, because He loves, can never agree that sin doesn't matter very much. It is precisely because sin matters so tremendously to God that Jesus dealt with it at such infinite cost to Himself. If sin is of little consequence to God, if the law doesn't matter, Calvary was a terrible mistake on God's part.

We don't need to take an "either-or" attitude toward grace and law, faith and obedience. Both are important. Trying to pit one against the other is like trying to decide which is more important to your automobile—the engine or the transmission, the tires or the steering wheel. You wouldn't get very far without all of them. Neither will you progress far spiritually without both grace and law, faith and obedience.

Perhaps the thing we need to be clear about is this: Grace and law have different purposes. One is not necessarily more important than the other, but each has its own special role to play in God's plan for us.

Through faith, we are saved by God's grace. That is its function. Law keeping can never save us. It was not designed for that, any more than the steering wheel was designed to carry the weight of your automobile on the street.

What, then, is the law's function? Paul says that it is "holy, righteous, and good" (Romans 7:12). We shouldn't feel that we have to take a negative attitude toward the law or obedience in order to be positive about the gospel.

The law functions as God's great standard by which to assess our relationship with Him. Jesus said, "If you love me, you will obey what I command" (John 14:15).

How much do you love Jesus? The proof will be in how willingly you demonstrate submission to His authority by obeying Him. The law is a yardstick by which we can measure our growth in grace—our progress in becoming like Christ.

Motive becomes the all-important consideration in this matter of obedience. If we are concerned about being victorious over sin in order to be saved, in order to deserve salvation, we have our motives all wrong. True obedience springs from a repentant, humble response to God's unconditional love. We obey Him, not so that He will save us, but in heartfelt gratitude that we *already enjoy salvation in Christ*! Obedience, no matter how correct, is as useless as the legalism of the Pharisees if it is born of anything other than sincere love for God. *Doing good things (and not doing bad things) for the wrong reasons is as unacceptable to God as disobedience itself. Both are manifestations of willful conduct and an unyielded will.*

We obey God because we love Him—pure and simple. Any other reason is the wrong motivation.

When we lived in Tegucigalpa, Honduras, our daughter Kathi came home from kindergarten with the product of her day's creative activities. It was an odorous can from which the dried residue of food announced it had been only partially washed. Under her teacher's tutelage, Kathi had glued macaroni and other pasta shapes to the can's exterior and then sprayed it with gold paint. Her fingerprints revealed that she had picked up the decorated can before the paint had dried completely. On entering the house, she proudly came to me and, with her face beaming with love, handed me her handiwork. As she skipped off, I wondered what price Kathi's precious gift would bring if sold in a fancy department store. Not much, I concluded. But what was it worth to me? It was priceless. Why was it so valuable? Its beauty? No. Its intrinsic value? No. It was the expression of Kathi's love that made my heart swell and my eyes brim.

As we come to God, some of us, like the Pharisees of old, are tempted to bring Him our obedience, expecting that its value will contribute to our salvation. We forget that our righteous deeds are worthless, "as filthy rags" (Isaiah 64:6, KJV). The value of our obedience is only found in our hearts broken in love to God, the motivation acceptable to God.

The law's function, then, is to serve as God's great standard by which we can assess our relationship with Him. But it seems clear that the relationship already has to be in place *before* the law can function. In other words, we can't really obey God unless we have a relationship with Him first. That's why true obedience must be motivated by love.

You see, God doesn't give His law to bad people in order to make them good. He gives His law to those He has already redeemed in order for them to show how much they love Him.

Notice what God said to the Israelites at Mount Sinai before He announced His law to them. "God spoke all these words: 'I am the Lord your God, who brought you out of Egypt, out of the land of slavery' " (Exodus 20:1, 2). Only after this introduction did He list His Ten Commandments.

Did God give His law, then, to the Israelites before or after He redeemed them? After. He already had delivered them from Egypt.

That is a significant point. The Ten Commandments were given to a people *who had already been redeemed*, not to a people *who were hoping to be redeemed*. God had already saved them. Then He told them how saved people ought to live. The purpose of the law is not to provide a way for us to be saved by obedience to it. Its purpose is to describe for us how we ought to live now that God has already saved us by His grace.

God's dealings with His people through both Old and New Testament times reveal that (1) we are saved by God's grace, not by our obedience to the law, and (2) those who have already been saved receive the law and obey it.

Paul puts it this way: "We maintain that a man is justified by faith apart from observing the law. . . . Do we, then, nullify the law by this faith? Not at all! Rather, we uphold the law" (Romans 3:28, 31).

Let's turn back to the question of how Jesus sets us free from our slavery to the law of sin. For even when we love Him, we still find ourselves, like the apostle Paul, struggling with this matter of sin and obedience, wanting to do right but finding ourselves doing wrong. We cannot free ourselves. Only Jesus can do that for us.

How does Jesus do it?

Usually, we try to free ourselves by making a mental check-list of our sins and then crossing them off as we quit doing them. The more sins we can eliminate from the list by superhuman effort, the more perfect we think we are. Finally, we will have everything crossed off the list and will no longer be doing anything sinful. We will be sanctified. That, I say, is how most of us approach this matter of obedience. We define goodness as avoiding badness.

But this approach causes several problems.

First, it suggests that the more sins we conquer, the more

perfect we become. And that the more perfect we are, the less grace we need. Eventually, according to this line of reasoning, we'll be so perfect we won't need any more grace. We'll be ready to be taken straight to heaven.

Second, what if we aren't successful at eliminating all the bad things on our list? Most of us find it difficult to do so, and the result is hopelessness and despair. After all, if good Christians should overcome sin in their lives, it's pretty discouraging when we try and fail.

Third, if we are successful in eliminating sins from our lives— or if we think we are—we tend to become modern versions of the Pharisee in Jesus' story who thanked God he was not a sinner like other men! It's so easy to develop inflated views of our own goodness and to build up ourselves by pointing out how bad everyone else is.

This approach—trying to be good by not being bad—does not result in confident Christians rejoicing in victory over sin through freedom in Jesus Christ.

Sins—defined as "bad acts"—really aren't the problem. They are only symptoms of the problem. The problem is *sin*—defined as a flaw in our natures, a bent to evil. Living in harmony with God's law, being Christlike, isn't simply a matter of no longer doing bad things. It's a matter of digging out the root of sin.

The real problem, you see, resides in our natures. Paul clearly considers his problem to be far more serious than simply the sinful acts he has committed:

> I know that nothing good lives in me, that is, in my sinful nature. . . . I see another law at work in the members of my body, waging war against the law of my mind and making me a prisoner of the law of sin at work within my members (Romans 7:18, 23).

In the Old Testament, the prophet Jeremiah also recognized that sin is rooted in the deepest core of our beings. He declared; "The heart is deceitful above all things and beyond cure. Who can understand it?" (Jeremiah 17:9).

You can identify with Jeremiah's question, can't you? Each of us, if we truly look deep within our hearts, will see evil thoughts and motives. I don't mean evil deeds that we would like to keep hidden from the prying eyes of others and from God. I mean evidence that our very natures are so sinful that we don't even recognize the seriousness of our condition. Sin isn't a bunch of deeds that we can fix, one deed at a time. Sin is a condition of the heart that reveals itself in our behavior.

So what can we do about it?

We can do nothing on our own: "Can the Ethiopian change his skin or the leopard his spots? Neither can you do good who are accustomed to doing evil" (Jeremiah 13:23). If you want to empty a room of darkness, you don't grab handfuls of darkness and start throwing them out the window. You turn on the light. The solution to sin in your life is to turn on the light, not to focus on trying to throw out sin.

If sin is just acts or behaviors, then it makes sense to try to fix it, one act at a time. But if sin is a disease, we must attack the disease, not just its symptoms. Victory over *sin* must come first, and that will lead to victory over *sins*. God isn't interested in tinkering with our lives and trying to patch them up. He's interested in giving us totally new lives.

So where do we find victory?

In a transplanted heart.

And where do we find a new heart?

A new heart can come only from God. He promises, "I will give you a new heart and put a new spirit in you; I will remove from you your heart of stone and give you a heart of flesh" (Ezekiel 36:26).

Once, God wrote His law on tablets of stone. Now, He wants to write His law in our minds and our hearts:

"The time is coming," declares the LORD, "when I will make a new covenant with the house of Israel and with the house of Judah. It will not be like the covenant I made with their forefathers when I took them by the hand to lead them out of Egypt. . . . This is the covenant I will make with the house of Israel after that time," declares the Lord. "I will put my law in their minds and write it on

their hearts. I will be their God, and they will be my people"
(Jeremiah 31:31-33).

The law once written in stone is to find a final resting place
in our minds and hearts. When that happens, when it becomes
a part of us, it will no longer be an external code that we must
try to obey contrary to our natural desires. Obedience will become a pleasure, the automatic response of our hearts to a God
of love. Jesus promises to change our natures if we will let Him.
He will transform us so that we will enjoy doing right. Sin no
longer will attract us. "I delight to do your will, O my God; your
law is within my heart" (Psalm 40:8, NRSV).

Our focus must not be simply on getting rid of sinful behavior or adding righteous deeds. We must focus on building a relationship with Jesus:

> All true obedience comes from the heart. It was heart
> work with Christ. And if we consent, He will so identify
> Himself with our thoughts and aims, so blend our minds
> and hearts into conformity to His will, that when obeying
> Him we shall be but carrying out our own impulses. The
> will, refined and sanctified, will find its highest delight in
> doing His service. When we know God as it is our privilege
> to know Him, our life will be a life of continual obedience.
> Through an appreciation of the character of Christ, through
> communion with God, sin will become hateful to us (Ellen
> White, *The Desire of Ages,* 668).

Yes, we believe, with the pioneers of this church, that those
who follow Jesus will "keep the commandments of God, and have
the faith of Jesus" (Revelation 12:17, KJV). We believe that even
more important than our obedience is the motive for our obedience. We obey because we love Him and because of His incredible grace.

Chapter 7

We Still Believe . . .
The Bible Is God's Inspired Word

William Miller did not base his conclusion that Jesus would return to earth "about the year 1843" on a superficial interpretation of a few texts in Daniel. He came to this conviction only after a two-year intensive study of the entire Bible and an attempt to harmonize its apparent contradictions. Miller's study method was simple. Starting at the first verse of Genesis, he began reading. He used no study aids or commentaries other than *Cruden's Concordance*. He moved from one text to the next only when he was satisfied that he had answered any apparent questions.

The fact that Miller was mistaken in his prediction of Jesus' coming doesn't necessarily mean that his method of Bible study was flawed. Protestants have historically believed that the Bible is its own best interpreter and that bringing together all it has to say about a particular subject will point to biblical truth. Of course, the thoughts of other Bible students and commentators can be valuable, but they cannot replace the authority of Scripture interpreting itself.

William Miller may have used a simple approach to his Bible study, but in his record book, he put down fourteen "rules of interpretation" that guided him in his study. They show he recognized a number of the difficulties we face in understanding the Bible's true meaning. He considered his last rule, number 14, to be the most crucial:

14. The most important rule of all is, that you must have

faith. It must be a faith that requires a sacrifice, and, if tried, would give up the dearest object on earth, the world and all its desires—character, living, occupation, friends, home, comforts, and worldly honors. If any of these should hinder our believing any part of God's word, it would show our faith to be vain (quoted in *These Times,* February 1974).

Here, William Miller put his finger on a key issue in our relationship to God and His Word. If we want to understand the Bible, we need to approach it in faith. We need to believe that God has spoken to us in the Bible. We need to believe that the Bible is His Word.

Ellen White comments:

The Bible is God's voice speaking to us, just as surely as though we could hear it with our ears. If we realized this, with what awe would we open God's word, and with what earnestness would we search its precepts! The reading and contemplation of the Scriptures would be regarded as an audience with the Infinite One (*Testimonies for the Church,* 6:393).

Miller's message was squarely founded on Scripture as the divinely inspired Word of God. Likewise, we Seventh-day Adventists, from the beginning, have based our beliefs on a "thus saith the Lord." We have rightfully declared that the Bible, and the Bible alone, is the only "infallible revelation of [God's] will. . . . The standard of character, the test of experience, the authoritative revealer of doctrines, and the trustworthy record of God's acts in history" (*Seventh-day Adventists Believe . . .* , 4). We have been characterized as "people of the Book" and have taken some pride in that description.

We must admit, however, that today, some of us Seventh-day Adventists, clergy and laypersons alike, are less "people of the Book" than we should be—and perhaps once were. Sadly, we are not generally depending today on the authority of Scripture as we have in the past, and we are suffering the consequences. We need to allow the Scriptures to take their rightful place as the foundation of our doctrines, the rule of our faith and practice, and the source of spiritual authority in our lives.

There is a divine power in the Bible that does not exist in other writings. This power comes from God Himself, because the Bible is His voice speaking to us through its pages:

> The word of God is living and active. Sharper than any double-edged sword, it penetrates even to dividing soul and spirit, joints and marrow; it judges the thoughts and attitudes of the heart (Hebrews 4:12).

Seventh-day Adventists today are reading many books and watching many videocassettes and listening to audio tapes of all descriptions. Many of these things are good, but we need to be drinking from the source rather than receiving our spiritual nourishment filtered through secondary means. Every one of us must personally engage in Bible study. Every pastor, every teacher needs to do the same and to preach and teach the Word on Sabbath mornings and in the classroom.

The most effective preaching is that which comes most directly from the Word of God. We can preach human ideas and philosophy. We can preach self-help, current-issues, and psychology-based sermons that may contain good thoughts. But unless we preach *biblical* sermons, sermons that create a hunger for the Word of God, our preaching will not have the power to change lives and bring men and women in contact with the living God.

The Bible itself claims to be God speaking to us. The apostle Paul affirms this when he commends the new Christians in Thessalonica for their faith: "When you received the word of God, which you heard from us, you accepted it not as the word of men, but as it actually is, the word of God, which is at work in you who believe" (1 Thessalonians 2:13).

Today, near the end of the twentieth century, there is much less certainty, even among many Christians, that the Bible is actually God's Word to humanity. The skeptical scrutiny that historical criticism has leveled at the Bible during the last century has taken its toll on faith. Polls show that the number of

Christians who say they believe the Bible to be God's Word remains high, yet the same polls indicate that Christians are reading their Bibles less and that Scripture is having a smaller impact on their daily lives.

According to the Princeton Religion Research Center, 85 percent of Americans believe the Bible is "inspired" in some sense, but only 39 percent agree that it is the "actual Word of God and is to be taken literally." The number of Americans who read the Bible outside religious services has declined, says the *National and International Religion Report*, to 34 percent in a typical week. Seventh-day Adventist Christians, unfortunately, are not immune to these same trends. Neglect of Bible study and increased doubts about its inspiration plague us as well.

The Bible is subject to attacks from many quarters in society. Perhaps the most prevalent opinion is simply to dismiss it. In our secular world, the great majority of people see the Bible as irrelevant, an ancient book with some historical and literary value, but with little or no connection to anything that is significant in their lives. Christians may not dismiss the Bible so completely, but far too many also feel the Bible is not particularly meaningful to real life. The result often is neglect.

Another characteristic of modern society is the almost subconscious rejection of authority. *Individualism* and *pluralism* are the watchwords of today's world. Such attitudes lead to distrust or rejection of any claim that the Bible is divinely inspired or has authority over our lives.

As well as by attacks from secular society, the role of the Bible has been weakened by attacks from within Christianity itself. In the 1800s (incidentally, about the same time William Miller was studying his Bible and the movement began that resulted in the founding of the Seventh-day Adventist Church), a number of Bible scholars began to apply prevailing ideas of rationalism and scientific inquiry to their study of the Bible. Approaching it as they would any other ancient historical document, they attempted to determine answers to "higher critical" questions, such as:

- What sources did the writer draw on, and how did he use

or combine them?

• What oral traditions underlie the present text?

• How did cultural and historical settings influence the written document?

• What literary categories can be identified?

• What evidence is there of editorial reworking of the material?

• How did the religious development of the community affect the written record?

These biblical scholars would certainly not have agreed with William Miller's principle that we must approach the Bible in faith if we are to understand it. Instead, they focused on the human element of God's Word, dissecting and analyzing it as they would an ancient Greek text of Homer. Throughout the rest of the nineteenth century and into the twentieth, their studies grew into elaborate hypotheses that carved up the Bible into a patchwork quilt of sources, speculations, and question marks—and virtually destroyed faith in its divine inspiration.

The result is that for many Christians today, the Bible is no longer *God's* Word, but *man's* word *about* God. It may *contain* the Word of God, but it is not itself God's Word. Such subtle distinctions may seem to be splitting hairs. However, when these scholars say that the Bible *contains* God's Word, they mean that the Bible is not God speaking to human beings, but human beings recording their search for God, for spiritual meaning. As we read of their search, we, too, may find God in our own time and way. In this way, the Bible contains God's Word for every generation. This is a far cry from what the Bible claims for itself. "All scripture is given by inspiration of God, and is profitable for doctrine, for reproof, for correction, for instruction in righteousness" (2 Timothy 3:16, KJV).

Higher criticism, now called historical criticism, has wreaked havoc with numberless Christians' faith in the Bible's divine inspiration. Yet we should recognize that some tools the critics use are legitimate if they are used with the proper presuppositions. A person who comes to the study of the Bible with the idea that it is a human document like any other ancient text may ask certain questions and use certain methods to arrive at conclusions that deny its divine inspiration. Yet a person who approaches the study of the Bible believing it to be truly inspired by God may ask the same questions and use the same methods to arrive at very different conclusions.

Some say, "In a more credulous age, it was easier to view the Bible as the almost audible voice of God speaking in our ears. Today, such an implicit trust in the Bible is naive and uninformed. If we're going to do justice to this ancient library of writings, we have to recognize the questions raised by historical, linguistic, and cultural factors. We have outgrown the early childlike faith of our spiritual forebears."

Is that true?

Actually, early Adventists were not unaware of the methods being applied to biblical interpretation. The nineteenth century was the heyday of scholarly theories regarding the Bible, and Adventists then understood the issues and the dangers these methods posed. Ellen White warns:

> The higher critics put themselves in the place of God, and review the Word of God, revising or endorsing it. . . . These higher critics have fixed things to suit the popular heresies of these last days. If they cannot subvert and misapply the Word of God, if they cannot bend it to human practices, they break it (*The Upward Look*, 35).

Yes, there are questions regarding the Bible that we cannot answer. There are problems that we cannot solve. The reason is that the written Word, like Jesus Christ, the living Word, is at the same time both divine and human. When Jesus came to earth as a human being, He became a unique God-man. In some way that we can never completely understand, His nature combined both the divine and the human into one new union.

Similarly, the written Word of God is also a mysterious blend of the divine and the human. Peter says, "Prophecy never had its origin in the will of man, but men spoke from God as they were carried along by the Holy Spirit" (2 Peter 1:21). Ellen White adds:

The Ten Commandments were spoken by God Himself, and were written by His own hand. They are of divine, and not human composition. But the Bible, with its God-given truths expressed in the language of men, presents a union of the divine and the human. Such a union existed in the nature of Christ, who was the Son of God and the Son of man. Thus it is true of the Bible, as it was of Christ, that "the Word was made flesh, and dwelt among us" (John 1:14) (*Selected Messages*, 1:25).

If the Bible is God's Word, it must come from outside our world, rather than springing from human creativity. It comes from God to inform, motivate, and change us, to tell us how we can be saved. Salvation does not originate with us. It comes from God. But it is worked out in our experience. Christ came from heaven, was born into the human family, and worked out salvation within human history. In the same way, divine thoughts have come to us through the minds of the prophets, who gave them expression. The Bible is fully human and also fully divine.

We cannot explain how Jesus could be both God and man at the same time, nor can we trace just how the divine and human elements interacted in His life. And the same is true of the unique combination of divine and human in the Scriptures. God spoke through human beings who lived at a particular place in a particular time. He communicated with humans who had limited communication abilities. Yet the result is *His* Word. Faith in the divine inspiration of the Bible doesn't mean that we have to deny or ignore its human aspects. We can hear God's voice in the Bible while at the same time recognizing the inevitable barriers God faced in communicating His Word in human language and culture.

There is something more important to a right understanding of the Bible than being able to find satisfactory answers to all the questions critics raise. Jesus said, "If anyone chooses to do God's will, he will find out whether my teaching comes from God or whether I speak on my own" (John 7:17). A willingness to hear and a willingness to follow are absolutely essential if we are to understand God's Word and allow it to speak to our lives today.

Many times, I've found people puzzling over some obscure text of the Bible, trying to unravel difficulties that have baffled Bible scholars for centuries, while willingly overlooking the extensive body of Scripture that plainly requires some unwelcome duty or condemns a pet practice. If we were more troubled by the texts we already understand and were less troubled by the texts we don't, perhaps we would come to understand all of the Bible better.

Of course, even the most transparent Bible passage contains unplumbed depths, and we certainly ought to be digging ever deeper into the Word. But isn't it true that the great majority of texts are plain? Isn't it true that we often fail to put into practice even the truth that we know? The problem usually isn't a lack of knowledge. The problem is more often an unwillingness to do what we know God's Word says we ought to do. Ellen White explains:

> Disguise it as they may, the real cause of doubt and skepticism, in most cases, is the love of sin. The teachings and restrictions of God's word are not welcome to the proud, sin-loving heart, and those who are unwilling to obey its requirements are ready to doubt its authority. In order to arrive at truth, we must have a sincere desire to know the truth and a willingness of heart to obey it. And all who come in this spirit to the study of the Bible will find abundant evidence that it is God's word, and they may gain an understanding of its truths that will make them wise unto salvation (*Steps to Christ*, 111).

With this, we are back to William Miller's vital rule number 14. "The most important rule of all is," Miller wrote, "that you must have faith." Possessing a Bible is of no value to us unless we spend time with it believing that it is God's revelation to us. Knowing something about the Bible, even knowing enough to prove doctrinal points, is of little value unless we believe that it is God speaking to us and unless we are willing to let His voice make a difference in the way we live. If we approach the Bible with faith and a willingness to bring our lives into harmony with its teachings, we will find the Christ-centered power that is waiting within its pages.

Can we once more deserve the title "people of the Book"? Let me urge and encourage you to begin today to let the Bible have a more prominent place in your spiritual life. Here are some practical suggestions:

1. Spend time with the Word. One of the chief excuses for lack of Bible study is "not enough time." I agree. Everyone's busy. Life today moves at a frenzied pace. But let me ask, "How many days has it been since you ate a meal?"

We manage to find time to eat food to sustain our bodies. We find time to go to the grocery store, buy food, bring it home, put it away, get it back out of the cupboard, prepare it, put it on the table, and eat it. Why? Because we're hungry and enjoy eating, because we know we cannot continue to live if we don't eat.

Can't we also recognize that feeding on God's Word is just as essential to our spiritual health as eating is to our physical health? Bible study takes time, but we find time for the things that are most important to us.

Only fifteen minutes a day spent in thoughtful, prayerful reading of the Bible will make a tremendous difference in your life. You will get to know the Author better. You will come to understand better how He wants you to live in order to be a happy and fulfilled Christian.

2. Have a specific time and place to study the Bible. Most people follow a daily routine. If you select a time of day when you are fresh and alert that provides an uninterrupted period for study—and devote that same time each day to Bible study— you'll find your Bible study both prioritized and rewarding. Similarly, picking a specific location to study makes it easier for you to get into a settled program of spending time with God's Word. But if a schedule doesn't work for you, the important thing is to take time daily for your Bible study.

3. Use a Bible translation that you feel comfortable with. Many of us grew up with the English King James Version (KJV) of the Bible. It's a beautiful translation that carefully tries to preserve the original Hebrew and Greek wording.

If a more modern translation leaves you cold, if it doesn't seem like "the Bible" to you, fine. Continue using your familiar KJV. But for many readers, the KJV is increasingly difficult to understand because the language is so unlike the way we speak today. Words have changed meanings. The *thees* and *thous* seem foreign, even confusing. Today, fewer than one in five Bible readers under the age of twenty-seven uses the KJV.

So if the KJV is hard for you to read, use one of the good modern translations. The New King James Version, the Revised Standard Version, and the New International Version are excellent translations in English. There are others. The Bible is God's voice to you for *today*.

4. Study to gain not only knowledge but also spiritual nourishment. Too often in our Bible study, we focus on interesting but insignificant details. Or we approach our study as a search for answers to questions of history, background, or authorship. Or we collect proof texts to support a certain idea. These things may be valuable in their place. But we need to approach the Bible first and foremost as a letter, a personal communication, from God to us. Head knowledge and heart knowledge need to go together.

Yes, the Scriptures are "profitable for doctrine" but also, and perhaps primarily, for "reproof, for correction, for instruction in righteousness" that we may be "perfect" (2 Timothy 3:16, KJV). The purpose of the Bible is to make us "wise unto salvation through faith which is in Christ Jesus" (verse 15, KJV).

In every passage, ask yourself, "What is God's lesson in this verse for me? What great difference will it make in my life?"

If we were to examine the Bible as we might analyze a chemical compound in the laboratory, it would appear to be like any other book—made up of paper, ink, and binding. The words are the same words used by other writers. We might conclude that nothing sets it apart from other books. Yet, there is a lifegiving power in the Bible that cannot be discerned by examination. It must be experienced. That power comes from its divine Author, from God Himself, who is the Source of all life.

The Bible has power, wonderful power, to change lives. Perhaps one of the best-known illustrations is how the Bible changed the lives of the colony founded on the island of Pitcairn by the mutineers from HMS *Bounty*. One of the fifteen men began brewing alcoholic drink, and soon the little colony was plagued by debauchery and vice. Within ten years, only one man, plus several women and children, were left. One day, the surviving sailor took the Bible from the famed *Bounty* chest. He read. He believed. He taught the others. When the colony was discovered years later, the community had changed drastically. It was prosperous. It had no jail, no alcoholic brews, and no crime.

Yes, the Bible has wonderful power to change lives—your life and mine.

Chapter 8

We Still Believe . . .
The Spirit of Prophecy Is God's Gift

On a December morning in 1844, barely two months after the Great Disappointment, Ellen Harmon, a sickly seventeen-year-old-girl with a third-grade education, went to visit Elizabeth Haines, a friend who had also expected Jesus to come on October 22. Three other women were there too. As the five women knelt in prayer, Ellen seemed lost to her surroundings. She later said that God had given her a vision concerning the travels of the advent people to the Holy City.

She describes what she saw:

> While I was praying at the family altar, the Holy Ghost fell upon me, and I seemed to be rising higher and higher, far above the dark world. I turned to look for the Advent people in the world, but could not find them, when a voice said to me, "Look again, and look a little higher." At this I raised my eyes, and saw a straight and narrow path, cast up high above the world. On this path the Advent people were traveling to the city, which was at the farther end of the path. They had a bright light set up behind them at the beginning of the path, which an angel told me was the midnight cry. This light shone all along the path and gave light for their feet so that they might not stumble. If they kept their eyes fixed on Jesus, who was just before them, leading them to the city, they were safe. But soon some grew weary, and said the city was a great way off, and they expected to have entered it before. Then Jesus would

encourage them by raising His glorious right arm, and from His arm came a light which waved over the Advent band, and they shouted, "Alleluia!" Others rashly denied the light behind them and said that it was not God that had led them out so far. The light behind them went out, leaving their feet in perfect darkness, and they stumbled and lost sight of the mark and of Jesus, and fell off the path down into the dark and wicked world below (*Early Writings*, 14, 15).

From this first vision was to come a prophetic ministry that would span more than seventy years, three continents, and a prodigious literary output. But in 1844, Ellen Harmon had none of the credentials to be taken seriously that she would later come to possess. She was young. She was uneducated and sickly. She had taken no prominent part in the Millerite movement. Besides, she was timid and extremely reluctant to share what God had shown her with the little band of advent believers in Portland, Maine. But after several attempts to avoid doing so, she hesitatingly told the group about her visions.

What caused this early band of believers to accept her visions as authentic? We may never know all the reasons, but apparently, they saw in Ellen's words light from God that encouraged them to believe He was still leading in their experience.

How open would the church be today to accept the visions of a seventeen-year-old girl as a legitimate manifestation of the biblical gift of prophecy? It would be much less open than were our pioneers, I'm sure. These disappointed believers were trying to sort through the events of the past few months. They were searching for something that would make sense of the disappointment they had suffered. So when, in God's providence, He began to communicate with them through young Ellen Harmon, they were willing at least to listen.

The Spirit of Prophecy was one of the first phenomena to arise in the post-October 22 setting, and it would prove to be one of the most cohesive factors among the little group that would eventually become Seventh-day Adventists. Acceptance of Ellen's visions was not immediate nor without difficulty. But within a year or two, there was general agreement that God was speaking through her to the scattered believers who were trying to salvage something from their advent experience. Ironically, Ellen White and her writings are, in some ways, more controversial in the church today, 150 years later, than they were then.

How can a church that claims to hold the Bible as the only "infallible revelation of [God's] will" (*Seventh-day Adventists Believe* . . . , 4) also believe that God has spoken to the church through the visions and writings of Ellen White? What is the relationship of her writings to the Bible?

Because we take the Bible seriously, we believe God has placed the gift of prophecy in His last-day church and that this gift was manifested in the life and work of Ellen White.

Jesus promised His disciples that when He returned to heaven, the Holy Spirit would serve as a living, ongoing Counselor, reminding them of Jesus' teachings, guiding them into all truth, and convicting the world of sin and judgment (see John 14:16-18, 25, 26; 16:5-16). This living Counselor, Jesus said, would remain with His people "forever" (John 14:16). The apostle Paul explains that the Holy Spirit bestows gifts upon the church in fulfillment of Jesus' promise:

> There are different kinds of gifts, but the same Spirit. . . . To one there is given through the Spirit the message of wisdom, to another the message of knowledge by means of the same Spirit, to another faith by the same Spirit, to another gifts of healing by that one Spirit, to another miraculous powers, to another prophecy, to another the ability to distinguish between spirits, to another, the ability to speak in different kinds of tongues, and to still another the interpretation of tongues. All these are the work of one and the same Spirit, and he gives them to each one, just as he determines (1 Corinthians 12:4-11).

Within the church, God has showered His followers with many talents so they can serve Him in a multitude of functions, as apostles, prophets, teachers, miracle workers, administrators, and linguists (see verses 27, 28). As Paul wrote to the Ephesians:

> It was he who gave some to be apostles, some to be prophets, some to be evangelists, and some to be pastors and teachers, to prepare God's people for works of service, so that the body of Christ may be built up *until we all reach unity in the faith and the knowledge of the Son of God and become mature, attaining to the whole measure of the fullness of Christ* (Ephesians 4:11-13, emphasis supplied).

Clearly, the gifts of the Spirit, including the gift of prophecy, are to be present in the church until the very end of time. The Bible itself lays the foundation for God to continue to speak to His people through modern-day prophets. If we reject the idea of the gift of prophecy in the church after Bible times, we are rejecting what the Bible itself plainly says will be the case.

Seventh-day Adventists have seen in Revelation 12:17 a description of their role as God's last-day remnant. That description gives two identifying characteristics of the remnant: they obey God's commandments, and they have the testimony of Jesus Christ.

What does the phrase *the testimony of Jesus* mean?

The testimony of Jesus can mean either the testimony others give about Jesus, which is the general testimony of the Christian church regarding Jesus, or the testimony Jesus gives, which is the testimony that Jesus Himself bears through the prophetic gift. I believe John intends the second meaning, because later, in Revelation 19:10, he defines "the testimony of Jesus" as "the spirit of prophecy." And a comparison of Revelation 19:10 with 22:9 indicates that those who bear the testimony of Jesus are also called "prophets."

Seventh-day Adventists, therefore, have seen these twin identifying characteristics of the remnant (see Revelation 12:17) as pointing to God's last-day people, who will obey all of the Ten Commandments and who will have in their midst the Spirit of Prophecy, the ongoing prophetic gift God promised to His church. We believe, just as did the pioneers of this church, that the prophetic gift was manifested in the life and work of Ellen White. We believe that God spoke to her and through her for the guidance of His remnant church.

What is the relationship of her writings, then, to the Bible? Can we honestly say that we accept the Bible alone as the infallible revelation of God's will?

Yes, Seventh-day Adventists base their beliefs on Scripture alone. While we believe that there is harmony between the Bible and the later gift of prophecy, we recognize that the Bible, and the Bible alone, is our rule of faith and practice.

We have already seen that the Bible plainly teaches that God has placed the gift of prophecy in His church until the very end of time. If we are going to accept the Bible as the infallible revelation of God's will, then we must accept that He has left the possibility of modern-day prophets in the church. To do otherwise is to deny Scripture itself.

How, then, are we to regard Ellen White's writings in relation to the Bible? Since both have the same Source, the Holy Spirit, are we to see them as equally authoritative? Are we to include her books along with the Scriptures as the foundation of our faith and practice?

In all honesty, we must admit that too many Seventh-day Adventists have done just that. In fact, some have placed *greater* emphasis on her writings than they have on Scripture. But that is not the position of the church, nor is that what Ellen White herself counsels us to do:

> God's Word is the unerring standard. The Testimonies are not to take the place of the Word. Great care should be exercised by all believers to advance these questions carefully, and always stop when you have said enough. Let all prove their positions from the Scriptures and substantiate every point they claim as truth from the revealed Word of God (*Evangelism*, 256).

> The Bible, and the Bible alone, is to be the rule of our faith. It is a leaf from the tree of life, and by eating it, by receiving it into our minds, we shall grow strong to do the

will of God. By our Christlike characters we shall show that we believe the word, that we cleave to the Bible as the only guide to heaven. So shall we be living epistles, known and read of all men, bearing a living testimony to the power of true religion (*Advent Review and Sabbath Herald,* 4, May 1897).

I recommend to you, dear reader, the Word of God as the rule of your faith and practice. By that Word we are to be judged. God has, in that Word, promised to give visions in the "last days"; not for a new rule of faith, but for the comfort of His people, and to correct those who err from Bible truth. . . .

The . . . . Lord desires you to study your Bibles. He has not given any additional light to take the place of His Word. . . .

The Spirit was not given—nor can it ever be bestowed—to supersede the Bible; for the Scriptures explicitly state that the Word of God is the standard by which all teaching and experience must be tested. . . .

Brother J would confuse the mind by seeking to make it appear that the light God has given through the *Testimonies* is an addition to the Word of God, but in this he presents the matter in a false light. . . .

The Word of God is sufficient to enlighten the most beclouded mind, and may be understood by those who have any desire to understand it. But notwithstanding all this, some who profess to make the Word of God their study are found living in direct opposition to its plainest teachings. Then, to leave men and women without excuse, God gives plain and pointed testimonies, bringing them back to the Word that they have neglected to follow (*Selected Messages*, 3:29-32).

Ellen White is clear that her writings are not to take the place of the Bible, be added to Scripture, nor be elevated above Scripture. They are "a lesser light" to point men and women to the "greater light" of the Bible (see *Colporteur Ministry*, 125).

The Bible explicitly claims to be the only authoritative standard of truth, the divinely inspired guide for Christians. No other message or writing can ever take the place of the Bible. It endures forever (see 1 Peter 1:25). It is truth and is the agent of Christian growth (see John 17:17). It points the way to salvation (see John 5:39). It is the weapon of the Christian in turning aside the devil's attacks (see Ephesians 6:17). It is the standard by which all who claim to have truth must be tested (see Isaiah 8:20). Therefore, we must measure the writings of Ellen White against the standard of the Bible, not vice versa.

Yet when we do so, we find in the Spirit of Prophecy an underlying harmony with Scripture. Her books are not to take the place of God's Word or even to be an addition to it. But her books and other writings, her ministry as the Lord's messenger to this church, have been of inestimable value. Her positive influence on the spiritual growth of the Seventh-day Adventist Church is beyond question.

What has it meant to the church and to each of us individually to have this manifestation of the prophetic gift in our midst? Consider the following:

1. Assistance in developing doctrines. We've examined in this book some of the major doctrines that the early believers hammered out in those days following 1844—doctrines that we still hold and share with the world. They didn't receive these doctrines as a result of revelations from Ellen White. They went to the Bible and dug them directly from the mine of truth. Yet the influence of her visions provided guidance so that right conclusions might be reached and substantiated. Ellen White never set herself up as a doctrinal authority through the prophetic gift. The leaders wrestled with Bible truth, and God guided them through her visions.

2. Protection against false teachings and fanaticism. One of the striking characteristics of these writings from the beginning has been their balance. In the formative years of the movement, before clear doctrinal positions had developed, there was serious danger of false teaching and fanaticism. The Spirit of Prophecy met these with a balanced view of truth that helped the pioneers avoid many problems. Today, her writings still guard from excesses and false doctrines.

3. Development of organization. As the church grew, organization was needed. Institutions were built. The work became more complex. Through all the growing pains, and particularly at the 1903 General Conference session, the Spirit of Prophecy gave practical guidance. The result is the worldwide church structure of today.

4. Plans for growth. Ellen White's visions have guided this church as it has developed solid, long-range planning for evangelism, medical and educational work, publishing, and other lines of gospel outreach. We have seen the fulfillment of God's promise, "Surely the Sovereign Lord does nothing without revealing his plan to his servants the prophets" (Amos 3:7).

5. Revelation of future events. Seventh-day Adventists have a perspective of the future that has been shaped by the great controversy theme as outlined by Ellen White. This detailed picture of the days ahead has given the church an added safeguard against the deceptions of Satan—deceptions that will increase as we approach the end.

6. Encouragement of Bible study. "In order to endure the trial before them, they [God's people] must understand the will of God as revealed in His word. . . . None but those who have fortified the mind with the truths of the Bible will stand through the last great conflict" (*The Great Controversy*, 593). Ellen White has consistently urged Seventh-day Adventists to a deeper study of God's Word.

7. Guidance in Christian living. God wants to reveal His love and grace to the world through the lives of those who claim to be His followers. Practical applications of the principles of Christian living form a large share of Ellen White's writings. She emphasizes principles as well as giving instruction in carrying out those principles.

Without these invaluable contributions from the Spirit of Prophecy, I suspect the Seventh-day Adventist Church wouldn't even exist. From the earliest days of this movement, Ellen White's pen and voice have counseled, guided, and led God's people to a deeper level of spiritual experience, to higher standards of personal living, and to clearer concepts of truth. Always, her words have uplifted Jesus Christ. Her writings encourage us to full acceptance of the gospel message by exalting the genuine deity and full humanity of Jesus Christ and the enormous significance of Calvary for the salvation of humanity.

In recent years, a critical attitude has arisen in the church toward this precious gift. Some have combed her writings, looking for flaws. Some have seized upon discrepancies and held them up as evidence for doubting that God has truly spoken through Ellen White to this church. This is extremely unfortunate.

Yet can we admit that some of this critical attitude has been a reaction to an unrealistic view of her writings that we have fostered in the church? Can we admit that over the years we have built up an image of Ellen White and her work that is unwarranted in many respects? Can we admit that often we have held her writings to a higher standard than we have demanded even of the Bible itself, that we have discounted the human element of her life and writings, until our faith has been shaken when we have had to face certain realities?

Yes, there are questions that can be raised about Ellen White and her work—just as we can raise questions about the Bible and its writers. Like the Bible writers, Ellen White was a human being with faults, although she was a staunch Christian woman. Like Bible writers, she sometimes misunderstood God's communications to her. Like them, she sometimes used uninspired sources to help her convey her message from God. Like them, she did not always acknowledge the sources she used. And, like the Bible, her writings contain discrepancies.

These concepts should not destroy our faith. When God communicates with us, He must filter His message through human channels—and anything humanity touches is liable to mistakes. God is perfect, but we humans are imperfect.

In spite of the questions that critics can raise, the proof is in the reading. When working in the Carolina Conference, I challenged the ministers, teachers, and office staff to read through the nine volumes of *Testimonies for the Church* in a single year. I accepted the challenge myself. The fifty of us who successfully completed the course found that reading these books was an enormous blessing. I am convinced that whoever comes to the Spirit of Prophecy sincerely will discover in these writings the hallmarks of divine inspiration. Many who reject her writings simply haven't read them.

I believe we can acknowledge the questions we may have about certain aspects of Ellen White and her writings while at the same time maintaining our faith in her role as a messenger for God, a genuine manifestation of the prophetic gift for God's end-time church. Shall we discard all the counsel, the light, the truth, the spiritual insights available to us in this precious gift simply because we cannot explain every question that may arise? That would be like refusing to fly on an airplane because we can't explain all the factors at work in aerodynamics.

Immediately after the Great Disappointment of 1844, God sent a vision to Ellen White to encourage His people to continue to hold fast their faith. I believe He is still encouraging us, through her writings, to hold fast our faith 150 years later. That first vision assured our spiritual forebears that if they continued to walk in the light that had been guiding them, they would at last arrive at the Holy City. I believe the same is still true.

If we continue to follow the light God has so graciously given us in His Word and in the Spirit of Prophecy, we will one day soon arrive at the New Jerusalem and see Jesus.

Some years ago, my father, while serving as evangelist in the New York Conference, invited to our home the leader of another religious denomination that also had its roots in the Millerite movement. This man had attended all but one of my father's evangelistic meetings. Sitting by the fireplace, the other minister wondered aloud why there was such a difference in the way the two churches, both founded in the Millerite movement, had grown through the years. He observed that both denominations share major fundamental beliefs, yet he wondered why his church had just a few thousand members and a few scattered congregations, while the Seventh-day Adventist Church was a rapidly growing, worldwide body. Dad simply said, "We trusted the messages of the little lady that God raised up to set our course."

Silent pondering was the man's response.

Chapter 9

We Still Believe . . .
God's Church Unites All Believers

You would think that Christians would be happy to hear that Jesus is coming soon. But as the Millerites quickly learned, people don't always rush to accept the good news. Although thousands gladly accepted Miller's message of Jesus' coming, many more thousands rejected it. Scoffers in the world were to be expected, but scoffers in the churches were more difficult to understand.

Miller didn't set out to establish a new church. He intended to warn the world of Jesus' coming from within the framework of existing denominations—sort of an interdenominational revival.

Yet inevitably, the message of Jesus' return caused ruptures with the established churches. The idea of a Jesus who would appear in a few months did not always agree with their doctrines. The positive effects of their members' revival from Miller's preaching looked less promising when the advent hope became more important to his followers than their denominational affiliation. Millerites, who ardently believed they must share the news of Jesus' soon return, found it increasingly difficult to fellowship in congregations that did not want them to continue agitating their new beliefs.

As the time approached when Miller and his followers believed Jesus would return, opposition in the churches grew more pronounced. Established congregations refused to allow Millerites to hold services in their buildings. Millerite preachers found themselves shut out of local pulpits. Preachers who became followers of Miller lost their jobs. And increasingly, advent believers who would not be quiet about their beliefs were disfellowshiped from their church homes.

Among these were Ellen Harmon and her family. Here's how she describes their experience:

> The Methodist minister made us a special visit and took the occasion to inform us that our faith and Methodism could not agree. He did not inquire our reasons for believing as we did, nor make any reference to the Bible in order to convince us of our error; but he stated that we had adopted a new and strange belief that the Methodist Church could not accept. . . .
>
> The next Sunday, at the commencement of the love feast, the presiding elder read off our names, seven in number, as discontinued from the church. He stated that we were not expelled on account of any wrong or immoral conduct, that we were of unblemished character and enviable reputation, but we had been guilty of walking contrary to the rules of the Methodist Church. He also declared that a door was now open, and all who were guilty of a similar breach of the rules would be dealt with in like manner (*Testimonies for the Church*, 1:41, 43).

In the face of such opposition, Millerites began to view the churches as "Babylon" and to call the faithful to "come out." Understandably, these early Adventists decided that those who opposed them with such hostile measures were actually opposing the Christ they preached.

Opposition intensified as October 22, 1844, approached. And following the Great Disappointment, the ridicule and pity of their former church friends was almost more than the bereft believers could bear. It's no wonder that they reacted by becoming highly suspicious of church organization. Their suspicion was strengthened by the scattered condition of the different groups and by the fact that they often had little doctrinal unity beyond their belief in the soon coming of Jesus.

By uniting with Miller's unpopular movement, our pioneers

had demonstrated their willingness to go against conventional wisdom. They continued to demonstrate this independent thinking by their suspicion of church organization. This was as true of that group which would later become Seventh-day Adventists as it was of other Millerite groups. Not until the early 1860s did circumstances overcome their reluctance to form a new church body. After a number of tentative organizational steps, delegates met in May 1863, in Battle Creek, Michigan, to draft a constitution for a general conference, marking the official organization of the Seventh-day Adventist Church.

Having been cast out of their churches because of their belief in the soon return of Jesus, the scattered advent believers just before and following the Disappointment looked to each other for spiritual support. Persecution and ridicule drew them together even more closely. A bit later, doctrinal isolation from Sunday-keeping Christians would do the same for those early believers who adopted the seventh-day Sabbath.

Thus one of the characteristics of the Millerites was their closeness to one another, their spiritual unity. With the world and the churches against them, they had no one else to cling to but to each other! They referred to themselves as the "scattered flock" or the "advent band." In her first vision, Ellen White mentions, in passing, the bonds of love that united these early advent believers. She describes God protecting His people from their enemies, and then she says, "The synagogue of Satan knew that God had loved us who could wash one another's feet, and salute the brethren with a holy kiss" (*Life Sketches*, 65).

One hundred fifty years later, we have a well-developed church organization. We have outgrown most of our fear of organization. But we have lost, also, it seems to me, too much of our sense of being one in Christ.

Just before His crucifixion, Jesus told His disciples, "My command is this: Love each other as I have loved you" (John 15:12). Then He prayed for the twelve and "for those who will believe in me through their message." And what was the burden of His prayer?

That all of them may be one, Father, just as you are in

me and I am in you. May they also be one in us so that the world may believe that you have sent me (John 17:21).

Jesus spent the final precious moments of His earthly life praying that you and I and all His people would be united in Him, united in our love for Him and for each other. Today, the Seventh-day Adventist Church is no longer a small band of believers in the northeastern part of the United States. We are a world church, rapidly approaching ten million members. We are in almost every country on earth. We speak and preach in hundreds of languages and dialects, live in diverse cultures, belong to many nations and races, and have different educational and economic backgrounds. But *we are all one in Christ!*

In spite of our differences, we have one great unifying bond that overshadows all else: *We are all brothers and sisters in Christ Jesus our Lord!* As I have traveled to various parts of the world to meet with our members, I have been impressed by the underlying unity that holds us as a church family together, no matter where we live or what our circumstances may be. We all love the same Jesus. We all believe the same truths. We all plan to live together one day soon in heaven.

It's as true today as it was when the apostle Paul wrote:

All of you who were baptized into Christ have been clothed with Christ. There is neither Jew nor Greek, slave nor free, male nor female, for you are all one in Christ Jesus (Galatians 3:27, 28).

We are all part of God's great family, and like all families, we have our disagreements at times. But *we remain part of the same family!* Oh, I wish we could all understand that better than we do! Our motto should be "Unity in Diversity." God doesn't expect us all to see things exactly alike. He doesn't expect us to lose our national, tribal, or racial identities. He doesn't expect us all to worship Him in precisely the same ways. But He does expect us all to love one another and to recognize that we all belong to His family:

A new commandment I give you: Love one another. As I have loved you, so you must love one another. All men will know that you are my disciples if you love one another (John 13:34, 35).

Consider those words of Jesus carefully. They are tremendously significant for the church today.

1. Jesus commands us to love one another. Love is not an option for a Christian! Does that surprise you? How can Jesus "command" us to love one another? Doesn't love, by its very nature, have to be spontaneous and freely given? We can't love on command, can we?

The love about which Jesus speaks is a principle. He isn't telling us that we have to have warm feelings of affection for all our brothers and sisters around the world—although I believe that the more we come to know each other, the more such feelings will occur. Jesus is talking about the kind of love Paul describes in 1 Corinthians 13.

Love, as we have come to think of it in much of the world today, is a debased currency. We say we love our husband or wife, our children, the dog, our new car, a new dress, a new recipe, a friend's hairstyle. We sometimes use the word to mean a sentimental feeling that makes our knees weak. At other times, we use it to mean we enjoy something that gives us pleasure. The fact is, we have overused the word until it means almost nothing.

The love Jesus is talking about and that Paul describes is something much stronger, much more permanent than our modern wishy-washy ideas of love. The love Jesus commands us to have for our brothers and sisters is patient and kind. It . . .

does not envy, it does not boast, it is not proud. It is not rude, it is not self-seeking, it is not easily angered, it keeps no record of wrongs. Love does not delight in evil but rejoices with the truth. It always protects, always trusts, always hopes, always perseveres. Love never fails (1 Corinthians 13:4-8).

These are all attributes that by the grace of God we can choose to exhibit toward others, and therefore Jesus is well within His rights to command us to have this kind of love for each other. Such love, Jesus says, is not optional for His people. If we are to be obedient to Him, we must have this kind of love.

2. We are to love each other in the same way that Jesus has loved us. This is a tall order. What kind of love did Jesus exhibit toward us?

This is how we know what love is: Jesus Christ laid down his life for us. And we ought to lay down our lives for our brothers. If anyone has material possessions and sees his brother in need but has no pity on him, how can the love of God be in him? Dear children, let us not love with words or tongue but with actions and in truth (1 John 3:16-18).

To love as Jesus loved! We can do that only when we allow His love to permeate our lives. "We love because he first loved us" (1 John 4:19).

Jesus' love for us was a love that resulted in action. He didn't consider His position in heaven something to cling to selfishly as long as He could save us by giving it all up. He emptied himself, "made himself nothing" (Philippians 2:7), in order that we might be made the righteousness of God in Him (see 2 Corinthians 5:21).

That is how we are to love one another, Jesus says. We must hold ourselves, our talents and abilities, our positions, and our possessions in readiness for service to each other. It isn't enough merely to say we love. Our actions must demonstrate that we love. The self-sacrificing spirit of Jesus must live in us for the good of others.

We can't generate such love in our own strength. It is beyond our power. Jesus has to do it for us. And He will—if we will allow Him to. Our part is to be willing.

3. This love will be a powerful witness for Jesus and His truth. "By this all men will know that you are my disciples, if you love one another" (John 13:35). The practical outworking of love in God's family will be the most powerful witness possible to the world that the claims of Christianity are true.

The world often has little interest in our doctrinal concerns. But the world is still impressed when someone shows disinterested love for others. In recent times, the world has honored people like Albert Schweitzer and Mother Teresa because they have exhibited the kind of love Jesus has said each of His followers should have!

Isn't it tragic that displays of such love are so rare? The Seventh-day Adventist Church should be filled with such examples.The world can argue with our theology. It can dismiss our message—and often does. But it cannot ignore the impact of our lives when we manifest disinterested love for others. Ellen White's familiar words come to mind:

> If we would humble ourselves before God, and be kind and courteous and tenderhearted and pitiful, there would be one hundred conversions to the truth where now there is only one. But, though professing to be converted, we carry around with us a bundle of self that we regard as altogether too precious to be given up. It is our privilege to lay this burden at the feet of Christ and in its place take the character and similitude of Christ. The Saviour is waiting for us to do this (*Testimonies for the Church*, 9:189, 190).

As others have pointed out, God's church should be a hospital for sinners, not a showcase for saints. If you have ever had to go to the hospital, perhaps to the emergency room, your main concern is to get help. You want the hurting to stop.

A friend of mine broke his back in an accident and in great pain was rushed to the nearest hospital. When he arrived, nurses and medical technicians in the emergency room sprang into action. Not one of them scolded him for being careless and breaking his back. Not one made him feel that he had disrupted his or her day by showing up at the hospital for treatment. They simply did what needed to be done to bring relief.

When the doctor arrived, he didn't enter into a medical discussion about bone structure or how fractures heal. He didn't blame my friend for the condition he was in—even though the accident had been his fault. The doctor gave him a large shot of Demerol and set about treating the fracture.

My friend came to the hospital because he was injured. He wanted the hurting to stop. I believe a great many people—members and nonmembers alike—come to our churches on Sabbath morning for the very same reason. They have been injured by sin, and they want the hurting to stop.

But do we apply the spiritual healing that will stop their pain? Or do we criticize them, instead, by pointing out that it's their own fault they are hurting? How often do we overlook their hurts in order to lecture them on one of our own spiritual theories? When we love as Jesus loved, we will truly be a caring church—and that love will be a powerful witness for Him.

In 1844, our pioneers came through an intensely emotional experience in expecting the imminent return of Jesus. As a result, they felt a bond with each other and with Jesus that transcended all their other differences. They wept together, prayed together, and studied their Bibles together until they began to understand their disappointment and to set their feet on solid doctrinal ground. Their love for each other carried them through their disorganized phase in which they distrusted formal church structure and shunned setting forth a statement of beliefs.

Today, we have organization in abundance. We have formulated a system of biblical truths that we believe God has given us to share with the world. But we need more love. We need the sense of unity and shared mission that our spiritual forebears felt as they proclaimed, "Behold the bridegroom cometh; go ye out to meet him!"

William Miller's movement existed only because of its message and mission—mistaken though that message was in setting a specific time for Jesus to come. Its message, based on Scripture, gave the movement its authority. Millerism was a mission-driven movement. Miller and his followers believed with all their hearts that they had a message people *must* hear.

The same must be true of the church today. The Seventh-day Adventist Church has never considered itself merely another denomination. As a people, we view our church and message as a fulfillment of prophecy. We believe we are a prophetic people.

The church exists only by virtue of its message and mission—and only to the extent that both are based on Jesus Christ.

Paul says, "No one can lay any foundation other than the one already laid, which is Jesus Christ" (1 Corinthians 3:11). He says, too, that God's household, His church, is "built on the foundation of the apostles and prophets, with Christ Jesus himself as the chief cornerstone. In him the whole building is joined together" (Ephesians 2:20, 21).

The very existence of the church in the world today implies the moral authority of Jesus over society. Of course, society is very uncomfortable with the concept of authority—particularly moral authority. So the church's message, mission, and foundation are all under attack today. But the biblical basis of the church's message is sound. Its mandate to proclaim the gospel is clear.

Why, then, is the church under such attack?

I believe the church is under attack because it is both succeeding and failing. It is making progress—inadequate though it is—in carrying the message to every nation, language, and race on earth. That angers the devil, and he arouses opposition from the world. At the same time, the church is failing by not bringing about a level of revival and reformation that God expects of His followers.

Finally, the church today is under attack from within as well as without. The church is made up of imperfect men and women. No wonder it makes mistakes. Leadership at every level is prone to err. Certainly, we make our share of mistakes at the General Conference! And some are quick to point to such mistakes as a reason to reject the authority of the church. Others point to failed organizational policies and use these failures as a reason to lose confidence in the church and its leaders. Such critics of the church use its failures as justification for setting up parallel organizations, that are, they suggest, more pure and error free. Yet in doing so, they operate outside the authority of the church. Clearly those who call for Seventh-day Adventists to leave the church and to join new organizations ignore the direct words of Ellen White:

The church may appear as about to fall, but it does not fall. It remains, while the sinners in Zion will be sifted out—the chaff separated from the precious wheat. This is a terrible ordeal, but nevertheless it must take place (*Selected Messages,* 2:380).

God is at the head of the work, and He will set everything in order. If matters need adjusting at the head of the work, God will attend to that, and work to right every wrong. . . . God is going to carry the noble ship which bears the people of God safely into port (ibid., 2:390).

When anyone is drawing apart from the organized body of God's commandmentkeeping people . . . when he begins to pronounce judgment against them, then you may know that God is not leading him (ibid., 3:18).

We cannot now step off the foundation that God has established. We cannot now enter into any new organization; for this would mean apostasy from the truth (ibid., 2:390).

Clearly, the proper response to administrative failures is not to abandon the church for alternative organizations. The proper response must be accountability exercised within the framework of the love Jesus commanded us to have for one another!

One hundred fifty years after 1844, we still believe Jesus is coming soon. We still believe the world needs to hear that He is coming. We still believe God selected William Miller to give that message in a special way. And we still believe that the Seventh-day Adventist Church stands in a direct line from Miller's movement with a prophetic mandate to proclaim the everlasting gospel in the light of Jesus' soon coming.

Organization, as imperfect as it may be, is essential to fulfilling Christ's mandate to take the gospel to all the world. Clear, biblical doctrine is vital. But the foundation underneath all must be Jesus Christ. Unless both our doctrine and our organization reflect Him, they will be hindrances, rather than aids, in fulfilling our mission. All of us, as members of His church, are standing on the same foundation. God's church embraces men and women, boys and girls, from nearly every nation of earth. We are all one body—His body:

The body is a unit, though it is made up of many parts; and though all its parts are many, they form one body. So it is with Christ. For we were all baptized by one Spirit into one body—whether Jews or Greeks, slave or free— and we were all given the one Spirit to drink (1 Corinthians 12:12, 13).

We are all under God's authority, and His authority is love. Here is the true basis of unity and power. "Let us love one another, for love comes from God. . . . Whoever does not love does not know God, because God is love" (1 John 4:7, 8).

Chapter 10

We Still Believe . . .
The Great Controversy Scenario
Is Real

Impossible!

Unbelievable!

During the last five years, incredible changes have kept our eyes and ears all but glued to our televisions and radios.

In 1988, the world seemed firmly locked in the icy grip of the cold war. The Soviet bear and the American eagle glared at each other over their stockpiles of nuclear weapons. East and West protected themselves by building more and better machines capable of destroying the entire world ten times, a hundred times, a thousand times, over.

Then the cold war began to thaw. Droplets of moisture formed, joined together, and began to drip from the ice that held the two superpowers in stalemate. The warm winds of change continued to blow, and rivulets trickled from the ice. The rivulets became streams, and the streams became torrents before our very eyes. Great chunks of ice began falling away, until it was difficult to keep track of the torrent.

Suddenly President Gorbachev and Pope John Paul II were conferring, then Gorbachev and President Bush, then Bush and President Yeltsin, then Yeltsin and the leaders of Europe, Japan, and China. Old alliances collapsed. New ones formed. The Berlin Wall crumbled as young people danced on its top and carried away chunks as souvenirs. Germany—East and West— reunited. Russia and the other Soviet republics went their separate ways. *Glasnost* and *perestroika* became part of everyone's vocabulary.

115

Soon, even Israelis and Palestinians stood on the White House lawn and extended their hands in peace.

Seldom in human history have such turnarounds in world affairs been more startling or sudden—or perhaps more prophetic. Pope John Paul II may have been more accurate than he realized when he referred to his historic meeting with Gorbachev in December 1989 as "a sign of the times, . . . a sign that is rich in promise." Gorbachev, in turn, acknowledged the pope as "the highest religious authority in the world." Said the then-Soviet leader, "Our time is indeed a watershed of destiny." One news report called the meeting a symbol of the end of the twentieth century's most dramatic spiritual war—the seemingly irresistible force of Communism battering against the immovable object of Christianity.

It may be too early yet to assess accurately what all these changes really mean. Are they permanent? What other changes will take place? Is true world peace just around the corner?

What does seem clear is that the world has radically changed and will never be the same again. Perhaps in light of all that has happened during the last few years, we should pay attention, again, to words written many years ago by Ellen White, who viewed world events from a prophetic perspective:

> In the annals of human history, the growth of nations, the rise and fall of empires, appear as if dependent on the will and prowess of man; the shaping of events seems, to a great degree, to be determined by his power, ambition, or caprice. But in the word of God the curtain is drawn aside, and we behold, above, behind, and through all the play and counterplay of human interest and power and passions, the agencies of the All-merciful One, silently, patiently working out the counsels of His own will (*Prophets and Kings*, 499, 500).

If current trends continue (and no one can be sure that they will), the world seems likely to experience a radical restructuring that could well set the stage for the final events of Bible prophecy.

Of course, the Bible doesn't precisely predict the rapid reforms taking place in the Communist world today. It doesn't tell us what the political map will be like next year. We cannot claim that a particular event in Eastern Europe fulfills a specific prophecy. But the Bible does predict, in broad terms, what the world will be like when the end comes—and it is a picture that fits much of what we see around us today.

People have always wondered what the future holds. The presidents and prime ministers of the world today are not the first. Thousands of years ago, another world political figure, Nebuchadnezzar, king of Babylon, also wished to look into the future. The Bible says that as he was lying on his bed, his mind turned to things to come. In Nebuchadnezzar's case, God saw fit to reveal to him, and to us, some specific information about the future and about the end of the world.

From our earliest days, Seventh-day Adventists have focused on the end time. That emphasis is evident in part of our name—Adventists. We are looking for our Lord Jesus Christ to come again, as He promises:

> Do not let your hearts be troubled. Trust in God; trust also in me. In my Father's house are many rooms; if it were not so, I would have told you. I am going there to prepare a place for you. And if I go and prepare a place for you, I will come back and take you to be with me that you also may be where I am (John 14:1-3).

So it's not surprising that early advent believers focused on Nebuchadnezzar's dream, as given in Daniel 2, to pinpoint their place in prophetic time. The multimetal image Nebuchadnezzar saw in his dream featured prominently in Millerite charts and preaching. The details are familiar to every Seventh-day Adventist: an image made of different metals that represented successive world empires, beginning with Nebuchadnezzar's own golden kingdom of Babylon. The four metals in the image represented four world empires that would follow one another. It has all happened just as God told Nebuchadnezzar it would.

But that was not the end of the king's dream or of the information that God wanted to give. It would be of little value to us today to know that God had predicted the rise and fall of world empires from Babylon to Rome. As Nebuchadnezzar was looking at the image in his dream, suddenly,

> a rock was cut out, but not by human hands. It struck the statue on its feet of iron and clay and smashed them. Then the iron, the clay, the bronze, the silver and the gold were broken to pieces at the same time and became like chaff on a threshing floor in the summer. The wind swept them away without leaving a trace. But the rock that struck the statue became a huge mountain and filled the whole earth (Daniel 2:34, 35).

Nebuchadnezzar's dream in Daniel 2 was a remarkable prophecy outlining world history in broad strokes centuries before the events occurred. Just as God foretold, the world has seen four world empires from Babylon to the present. Not five, not three, not six—but four.

The prophecy assures us that God knows the future and that He *controls* the future. The important aspect of Nebuchadnezzar's dream for us today is not that it explains the succession of world empires but that God will take events into His own hands and set up His everlasting kingdom. The rock that struck the image and grew to fill the whole earth was cut out of the mountainside "*not by human hands*" (verse 34, emphasis supplied).

The astonishing changes taking place in our world today may appear to be the result of human politics and economic forces. But behind all the play and counterplay of human history, the prophecy of Daniel shows us the unseen hand of God carefully orchestrating His own eternal purposes.

A democratic society that recognizes and promotes freedoms, including the freedom of religion, is infinitely preferable to a repressive, totalitarian society that denies basic human rights. For this reason, we rejoice that hundreds of millions of people are enjoying newfound freedoms. But neither democracy nor communism nor socialism is God's system. His eternal kingdom is built on different principles and will supersede all earthly governments and powers.

Do these startling world changes have any significance, then, in light of Bible prophecy?

Yes, because of these changes, it seems likely that world conditions are moving to reflect more closely the kind of situation the Bible suggests will be in place when God sets up His eternal kingdom.

According to the Bible, the great issue at the end of time will not be a conflict between democracy and socialism or between political or economic systems. It will be a conflict between good and evil. All the kingdoms of the world will be arrayed in a vast, unified block against those who remain faithful to God (see Revelation 13:1-8; 18:1-10). Religious forces, too, will be on one side or the other.

Yet for nearly a half century since World War II, the nations of the world have been united on practically nothing. The major constant in international relations has been the cold war between East and West. Now it seems possible that just as the Berlin Wall has come crashing down, so will all manner of other walls that divide peoples.

All these trends appear to be setting the stage for a worldwide confederacy of political and religious powers such as the end-time prophecies bring to view. It seems increasingly possible that a time of "peace" is at hand. And the Bible says that it will be at just such a time that the rock will strike the kingdoms of this earth and destroy them.

"You know very well," Paul writes, "that the day of the Lord will come like a thief in the night. While people are saying, 'Peace and safety,' destruction will come on them suddenly" (1 Thessalonians 5:3).

What does all this mean? It means that we are living in the toes of the image described in Daniel 2 and that the next great event in world history will happen when God sets up His kingdom that will last forever.

And, meanwhile, how should we spend our time?

Paul counsels us:

Our salvation is nearer now than when we first believed. The night is nearly over; the day is almost here. So let us put aside the deeds of darkness and put on the armor of light. . . . Clothe yourselves with the Lord Jesus Christ (Romans 13:11, 12, 14).

The Seventh-day Adventist Church arose out of an intense "end-time" experience in which the pioneers expected to see Jesus coming in the clouds on a specific day. That experience not only became the spiritual lens through which they viewed all subsequent events but also shaped the spiritual perceptions of Seventh-day Adventists ever since. We have, in a very real sense, never abandoned our expectation that Jesus is coming soon. From the very beginning, we have had an end-time focus.

Gradually, the belief in a soon-coming Saviour became incorporated into a larger perspective that Seventh-day Adventists refer to as "the great controversy theme." Although the outlines, as we have seen, are clearly present in the Bible, Ellen White was most instrumental in giving definition to this perspective. In 1858 she received a two-hour vision recapping material that had actually been given to her ten years earlier. She describes it this way:

In the vision at Lovett's Grove [Ohio], most of the matter which I had seen ten years before concerning the great controversy of the ages between Christ and Satan, was repeated, and I was instructed to write it out. I was shown that while I should have to contend with the powers of darkness, for Satan would make strong efforts to hinder me, yet I must put my trust in God, and angels would not leave me in the conflict (*Life Sketches*, 162).

On the way home following this vision, Ellen White suddenly felt a cold shock strike her heart and pass over her head and down her right side. She was insensible for a time and after recovering consciousness was not able to use her left arm or leg. She pressed on anyway and began writing out the vision.

At first she could write only a page a day and had to rest

three days before having strength to write more. But as she continued, she grew stronger until the effects of the shock finally disappeared. She was shown in a later vision that by the sudden attack, "Satan intended to take my life, in order to hinder the work I was about to write; but angels of God were sent to my rescue" (ibid., 163).

Ellen White literally spent her entire life writing and rewriting the account of that vision that outlined the great controversy between Christ and Satan. In September of that same year, 1858, her 219-page book, *Spiritual Gifts—the Great Controversy Between Christ and His Angels and Satan and His Angels*, was published. Over the years, she expanded the work until it took the form we have today in the five volumes of the Conflict of the Ages series.

The great controversy between Christ and Satan began in heaven. As Revelation 12:7 tells us, "There was war in heaven. Michael and his angels fought against the dragon, and the dragon and his angels fought back." The struggle moved from heaven to Eden, continued to form a background to the history of humanity during succeeding centuries, and will be resolved only at the end of time, when Satan and all sinners will be destroyed.

The great-controversy perspective provides a context in which we can understand the tragedies, the cruelty, and the pain, misery, and suffering that exist wherever we look. Some of the most troubling moral questions in people's minds—religious and nonreligious alike—are "Why do pain and suffering exist? And why do bad things happen to good people?"

The great-controversy perspective also allows us to understand that God is not responsible for evil and suffering. Lucifer, a perfect, holy angel, perverted his God-given powers and became Satan, the adversary. The sin and misery we see in our lives and in the lives of others are all part of Satan's ongoing warfare against God. We and our world are caught up in a much larger struggle, a cosmic conflict that affects the entire universe.

In a real sense, the controversy was won by Christ on the cross. There, Satan was defeated and his kingdom doomed. That's why Jesus cried out, " 'It is finished' "(John 19:30). But

Satan, though vanquished, fights on. The final resolution of the conflict will come only at the end of time.

There are greater issues at stake in this controversy than simply our personal salvation or even the fate of our lost little planet. As important as these are, the larger issue is the question of God's character and the stability of His government. God must be vindicated. He must not only do right in meeting Satan's accusations, but also *be seen* by the universe to do right. For that reason, God allows the conflict to continue until it can be put to rest for all eternity.

God is vindicated precisely because of the way He has chosen to deal with sin. The history of the conflict between good and evil, from the time it began in heaven to the final overthrow of Satan's rebellion, is a demonstration of God's unchanging love.

Thus, how God has handled our salvation becomes a primary factor in establishing His character in answer to Satan's accusations. Lucifer charged God with being selfish and uncaring about the welfare of angels and other beings. He accused God of being unwilling to relinquish His position in any way to meet what Lucifer claimed were just demands. In short, he argued that God would not sacrifice any of His power or position.

Yet that is exactly what God did. He emptied Himself, made Himself nothing, and was born as a helpless human baby in order to meet the challenge of sin that Lucifer had unleashed upon the universe. He placed Himself in Satan's hands to live as a human. He allowed sin to take His life. And in so doing, He not only worked out our salvation; He forever put to rest Satan's accusation that He was not willing to sacrifice Himself for the good of His creatures. No wonder Jesus cried out, " 'It is finished!' " as He died on the cross.

The great-controversy theme directs our attention beyond the cross to the grand climax at the end of time. The Seventh-day Adventist scenario of those tumultuous last days includes a time of trouble "unequaled from the beginning of the world" (Matthew 24:21). There is no question that the Bible presents such a time. The last days will be perilous, with persecution culminating in a death decree. It will be a testing time that will prove our loyalty to God.

Yet I believe too many Seventh-day Adventists fear the end time so much that they lose sight of the fact that it means deliverance. After describing the anguish and terror that will prevail because of what is happening in the world in the last days, Jesus says, "When these things begin to take place, stand up and lift up your heads, because your redemption is drawing near" (Luke 21:28).

We are to welcome the end time, not fear it. Jesus assures us, "Surely I will be with you always, to the very end of the age" (Matthew 28:20). Does this mean that He will be with us only until the perils of the end time? Is Jesus going to abandon us in the time of trouble?

Never!

He promised to be with us all the way through to the kingdom, when we will see Him face to face.

We may fear the time of trouble because we believe that we will somehow have to rely on ourselves during that time, that Jesus will leave us to get through the best we can, that we will have to be able to summon up incredible reserves of spiritual and physical strength in order to stand.

It's true that the time of trouble will require much of us. I would not suggest that it will be easy. After all, the Bible calls it a "time of *trouble*." But I have good news. We will not have to face it alone. Jesus will walk with us through that dark valley, and we will safely walk through the shadows if we hold tightly to His hand.

In Ellen White's first vision, she saw the advent people on a narrow, high path leading to the Holy City. Behind them was a bright light, which shone along the path and represented the Millerite message of Jesus' soon return. As long as they kept their eyes on Jesus, the light illuminated their way. When they lost sight of Him, the light went out, and they stumbled and fell off the path.

In earth's darkest hour, the issue for you and me will be the same. Will we keep our eyes on Jesus? That is the whole question. We will pass through the perils of the last days in the very same way we face the perils of today—in the strength of Jesus and by trusting Him daily. Our standing with God after the close of probation—our assurance of salvation in the time of trouble—will be grounded on exactly the same foundation as it is today: salvation through faith in the righteousness of Jesus and in His grace and saving power.

I believe two questions face you and me as we look ahead to the end time:

• Are we developing a relationship with Jesus that can endure the trials and perils of earth's darkest hour, when every visible, human support is removed?

• Are we maintaining our experience of salvation in Christ, staying close to Him day by day, asking Him to convict us of sins we need to confess, coming to Him for the transformation of heart that we need to overcome our sins?

This is the relationship that we need to have with Jesus in order to face the end time with confidence in Him. If we are walking with Him by faith today, we will keep right on walking with Him through the time of trouble and into the kingdom. He will never leave us or forsake us.

The great-controversy theme also assures us that all sin ultimately will be destroyed. At the end of the great drama of the ages, Jesus will establish a new heaven and a new earth, new in the sense that our earth will be completely purged of everything that is the result of sin. The contrasts between the old and the new are striking:

• Genesis speaks of the creation of the world. Revelation speaks of the re-creation of the world (Genesis 1 and 2; Revelation 21:1).

Genesis tells of paradise lost. Revelation tells of paradise restored (Genesis 3; Revelation 21).

• Genesis describes the serpent as being victorious over humanity. Revelation describes the serpent being destroyed (Genesis 3:1-13; Revelation 12:9-11; 20:10).

• Genesis recounts how Adam and Eve tried to flee from God because of their sins. Revelation recounts how God and humans will live together for eternity (Genesis 3:8, 9; Revelation 21:3).

• Genesis portrays how Adam and Eve were barred from the tree of life. Revelation portrays how the redeemed freely will eat its fruit (Genesis 3:17; Revelation 22:2).

• Genesis shows God pronouncing the curse because of sin. Revelation reveals, "There shall be no more curse" (Genesis 3:14; Revelation 22:3).

• Genesis says we must live by the sweat of our brows. Revelation says we will live forever with God's name in our foreheads (Genesis 3:19; Revelation 22:4).

• Genesis tells how Adam and Eve forfeited their dominion over the earth and its creatures. Revelation tells how Adam and his descendants "shall reign for ever and ever" (Genesis 3:17; Revelation 22:5).

In beautiful words, Ellen White concludes the story:

The great controversy is ended. Sin and sinners are no more. The entire universe is clean. One pulse of harmony and gladness beats through the vast creation. From Him who created all, flow life and light and gladness, throughout the realms of illimitable space. From the minutest atom to the greatest world, all things, animate and inanimate, in their unshadowed beauty and perfect joy, declare that God is love (*The Great Controversy*, 678).

"Come, Lord Jesus" (Revelation 22:20).

The day He didn't come
Millennial Fever
by George Knight

October 23, 1844. One day after the faithful were to have gone home to heaven with Jesus. But Jesus didn't come, and the advent believers felt chained to the earth, reeling in shock and grief.

It is now fifteen decades after the great disappointment, and Jesus still hasn't come. Ever-deepening disillusionment

and skepticism crowd the minds of many. But somewhere between white-hot millennial fever and hope grown stone cold is the patience of the second-advent saints. This book shows how to find it.

US$14.95/Cdn$20.95. Paper.
US$19.95/Cdn$27.95. Hardcover.

To order, call toll free 1-800-765-6955, or visit your local ABC.